Civic Education and the Future of American Citizenship

Civic Education and the Future of American Citizenship

Edited by
Elizabeth Kaufer Busch
and
Jonathan W. White

LEXINGTON BOOKS
Lanham • Boulder • New York • Toronto • Plymouth, UK

Published by Lexington Books
A wholly owned subsidiary of The Rowman & Littlefield Publishing Group, Inc.
4501 Forbes Boulevard, Suite 200, Lanham, Maryland 20706
www.rowman.com

10 Thornbury Road, Plymouth PL6 7PP, United Kingdom

British Library Cataloguing in Publication Information Available

Library of Congress Cataloging-in-Publication Data

Civic education and the future of American citizenship / edited by Elizabeth Kaufer Busch and Jonathon W. White.
 p. cm.
Includes bibliographical references and index.
ISBN 978-0-7391-7056-4 (cloth : alk. paper) — ISBN 978-0-7391-7057-1 (pbk. : alk. paper) — ISBN 978-0-7391-7058-8 (electronic) (print) 1. Civics—Study and teaching—United States. 2. Citizenship—Study and teaching—United States. 3. United States—Politics and government—Study and teaching. I. Busch, Elizabeth Kaufer, editor of compilation.
LC1091.C52877 2013
370.11'5—dc23
2012035893

♾™ The paper used in this publication meets the minimum requirements of American National Standard for Information Sciences Permanence of Paper for Printed Library Materials, ANSI/NISO Z39.48-1992.

Printed in the United States of America

Contents

Acknowledgments

This volume is the product of much collaboration at Christopher Newport University. It was born out of a conference hosted by the Center for American Studies in February 2010 entitled "Civic Education and the Future of American Citizenship." Many of the contributors in this volume participated in that conference.

We thank CNU's president Paul S. Trible, who continues to carry out his vision to build a true liberal arts university; Provost Mark Padilla for his strong support of the Center for American Studies and its programming; Dean Bob Colvin for his leadership in developing the American Studies program at CNU and for guidance in the Center's work; Professors Ben Redekop, Brent Cusher, and Nathan Harter of the Department of Leadership and American Studies, for discussing the ideas found in this book with us as we've been working on it over the past few semesters.

We thank current and former CNU students Justin Lehman, Meghan Butler, Kat Forbes, Maddie Popham, Ashley Blatt, Ben Coffman, Erin Bello, and Kelsey Nichols, as well as our former administrative assistant, Krista Rogers, for assistance in research and the preparation of this book. Jesse Spencer, CNU's InterLibrary Loan specialist, tracked down numerous books and articles.

We thank the Jack Miller Center and the Thomas W. Smith Foundation for their sustained support of the Center through funding for lectures, conferences, student internships, and postdoctoral fellowships.

We thank Alison Northridge, Melissa Wilks, and Jehanne Schweitzer of Lexington Books, and Joseph Parry, our first editor at Lexington, for seeing this project to completion.

We thank Matthew Mendham and Bill McClay for commenting on the introduction.

Finally, we thank Nathan Busch for his tireless work in support of the Center, and his being a loving husband (to one of us) and drinking partner (to the other).

Introduction

Elizabeth Kaufer Busch and Jonathan W. White

America was founded with the understanding that its citizens would perpetually have to be educated in the nation's first principles in order for the republic to survive and its citizens to flourish. When John Adams wrote the Declaration of Rights of the Massachusetts Constitution of 1780—which is the oldest functioning written constitution in the world— he declared: "A frequent recurrence to the fundamental principles of the constitution, and a constant adherence to those of piety, justice, moderation, temperance, industry, and frugality, are absolutely necessary to preserve the advantages of liberty and to maintain a free government." Adams borrowed this idea—and much of this language—from George Mason's Virginia Declaration of Rights of 1776. It might seem strange today that such a declaration of *responsibility* would be found within declarations of *rights*, but Mason and Adams placed these clauses in their respective state constitutions to remind "the people" that their rights would only survive if "the people" remained vigilant and worthy of their rights. Indeed, Adams's constitutional provision went on to say that only by paying "particular attention to all those principles" could "the people" hold their elected officials accountable—"for the good administration of the commonwealth."[1]

Modern critics of the American founding rightly point out that "the people" meant something different in the 1780s than it means today. To be sure, in the early republic the vast majority of Americans were excluded from both the rights and responsibilities of citizenship. Virtually all women were denied the rights to vote and to own property. African Americans were also disfranchised in most states. Even poor, property-less white males could not vote in many states.[2] Yet the Declaration of Independence pointed toward a better future. It declared that all men— by implication, all human beings—possessed "certain unalienable rights, among which are life, liberty, and the pursuit of happiness."[3] "This they said, and this they meant," declared future president Abraham Lincoln in 1857. "They meant simply to declare the *right*, so that the *enforcement* of it might follow as fast as circumstances should permit. They meant to set up a standard maxim for free society, which should be familiar to all, and revered by all; constantly looked to, constantly labored for, and even

1

though never perfectly attained, constantly approximated, and thereby constantly spreading and deepening its influence, and augmenting the happiness and value of life to all people of all colors everywhere."[4]

The original Constitution contained mechanisms—such as the judiciary and the amendment process—through which the participation of the public and the exercise of fundamental rights could be broadened. Indeed, former slave Frederick Douglass urged that the Constitution, "interpreted as it ought to be interpreted, . . . is a GLORIOUS LIBERTY DOCUMENT." Despite the numerous injustices that had plagued America since the conclusion of the Revolutionary War, Douglass insisted that the principles were true and good and that the words of the document must be interpreted in a manner that inclined toward justice. "Read its preamble, consider its purposes. Is slavery among them? . . . if the Constitution were intended to be, by its framers and adopters, a slave-holding instrument, why neither slavery, slaveholding, nor slave can anywhere be found in it."[5] Foremost among the goals listed in the Preamble is to "establish justice." As the institution of slavery was unjust and therefore inconsistent with the universal human rights listed in the Declaration and protected by the Constitution, neither of these documents, in Douglass's view, perpetuated such an evil. On the contrary, the principles articulated by each paved the way for slavery's ultimate extinction.[6]

Both Lincoln and Douglass argued that the principles of the Declaration and Constitution should not be impugned simply because they have not been actualized. The principles contained in the documents are not hypocritical; rather, the attempt to bring them into practice has been imperfect and at times unjust. Nevertheless, the goal of liberty is worth pursuing and American history has been a story of the perpetual expansion of liberty to new groups of people.

But how could this liberty be protected for perpetuity? How could Americans secure the guarantees of liberty to themselves and their posterity? Through vigilance, according to James Madison. All citizens must jealously guard against any "experiment on our liberties." This "prudent jealousy," Madison adds, is "the first duty of Citizens, and one of the noblest characteristics of the late Revolution." Though jealousy and suspicion are not typically considered virtuous traits, in the American context of consent-based self-government they become *noble*. "The free men of America did not wait till usurped power had strengthened itself by exercise, and entangled the question in precedents. They saw all the consequences in the principle, and they avoided the consequences by denying the principle. We revere this lesson too much soon to forget it."[7] The lesson to which Madison refers is the duty to uphold the principles articulated in the Declaration that initiated the Revolutionary War.

Madison's words might today fall on deaf ears as America's youth are largely forgetting the lessons of the Founding era. A recent study found that 38.4 percent of Americans between the ages of 18 and 24 think the

Constitution should be replaced even though only 27.8 percent have actually read it![8] Moreover, a recent study indicates that America's office holders are proving themselves to be even less knowledgeable about civics than the average citizen.[9]

Nevertheless, the Constitution continues to be the law of the land—a law that demands allegiance regardless of whether citizens affirm its sentiments with rational awareness or passively ignore them. But what does it mean to govern ourselves under a document whose content is not read, whose purpose is not understood, and whose current meaning is no longer scrutinized by the wider public?

Madison's recommendation of "prudent jealously" assumed two important characteristics of rank and file citizens—prudence, or practical wisdom, and principle, or awareness of the rights and responsibilities of free citizens. While these traits may have characterized many of the leaders of the Founding era, an additional support would be needed to ensure their continuation and expansion moving forward so that Americans' vigilance would not be ignorant or dangerous. The proposed remedy was to make education available to all Americans.

Many in the Founding generation, including George Washington, Thomas Jefferson, Benjamin Franklin, and later Abraham Lincoln, promoted the idea of an educated public as the cornerstone of a functioning republic. Franklin recommended the proper education of the youth as the "surest Foundation of the Happiness both of private Families and of Common-wealths." Only through such knowledge can citizens insulate themselves against the "mischievous Consequences that would attend a general Ignorance among us."[10]

Concern for such "mischievous Consequences" led many prominent statesmen to promote the fostering of an educated public as one of government's foremost responsibilities. Upon leaving the presidency, Washington admonished Americans to promote "as an object of primary importance, institutions for the general diffusion of knowledge." He recognized that the unique "structure of [American] government gives force to public opinion" which makes it "essential that public opinion should be enlightened."[11] Similarly, Thomas Jefferson warned that without the safeguard of publicly funded education even the freest of republics could degenerate into despotism. His 1778 proposal for public education in Virginia cautioned that "even under the best forms, those entrusted with power have, in time, and by slow operations, perverted it into tyranny." Jefferson's Enlightenment philosophy, which informed his authorship of the Declaration, recognized the inclination of humans toward self-aggrandizement. Whereas ruthless ambition may take many forms, even in a free republic, it cannot be eliminated. Jefferson was quite candid that "the most effectual means of preventing this would be, to illuminate, as far as practicable, the minds of the people at large."[12] Similarly, Lincoln recognized the same threat when he warned against the rise of "an Alexander, a Caesar, or a Napoleon"—that is, "some man possessed of the loftiest genius, coupled with the ambition to push it to its utmost stretch" in America. His remedy, like Jefferson's, was to provide an education for "the people to be united with each other, attached to the government and laws, and generally intelligent."[13]

"Upon the subject of education," said a young Lincoln in 1832, "I can only say that I view it as the most important subject which we as a people can be engaged in. That every man may receive at least, a moderate education, and thereby be enabled to read the histories of his own and other countries, by which he may duly appreciate the value of our free institutions, appears to be an object of vital importance, even on this account alone, to say nothing of the advantages and satisfaction to be derived from all being able to read the scriptures and other works, both of a religious and moral nature, for themselves." For Lincoln, general education and civic education were virtually synonymous. And such an education had several purposes. It taught people to appreciate their nation and their history; it taught them how to be citizens of a free nation; and it would give them satisfaction and pleasure when they exercised the freedom to read and understand and appreciate the life of the mind. "For my part," Lincoln concluded, "I desire to see the time when education, and by its means, morality, sobriety, enterprise and industry, shall become much more general than at present."[14] Education and civics, for Lincoln, would lead to a virtuous citizenry, just as George Mason and John Adams hoped that it would.

Lincoln's devotion to the idea of civic education for all Americans was rooted in his belief that such education was necessary to create a people who would preserve the nation. Lincoln was not interested in preserving the nation—or its institutions—solely for the sake of the Union. He believed that American institutions were worth preserving because they preserved liberty.[15] Like George Mason and John Adams before him, Lincoln believed that Americans needed to force themselves to remember the lessons of the American Founding. In the 1830s, as American society seemed to be descending into a dark age of mob violence and anarchy, the lessons of the Founders appeared to be largely forgotten. Lincoln proposed a "simple" solution: "Let reverence for the laws, be breathed by every American mother, to the lisping babe, that prattles on her lap—let it be taught in schools, in seminaries, and in colleges;—let it be written in Primmers, spelling books, and in Almanacs;—let it be preached from the pulpit, proclaimed in legislative halls, and enforced in courts of justice. And, in short, let it become the *political religion* of the nation; and let the old and the young, the rich and the poor, the grave and the gay, of all sexes and tongues, and colors and conditions, sacrifice unceasingly upon its altars."[16]

Jefferson, Franklin, Washington, and Lincoln would agree that the very exceptionalism of the American experiment creates the need for civic education, the purpose of which is to develop young, reflective, rational citizens who can thrive in and perpetuate American civilization. Unfortunately, America's youth today seem to lack adequate opportunities, if not also the ability or will, to examine critically the foundations of this nation. Concern with civic illiteracy led to a national task force that called "on the nation to reclaim higher education's civic mission." In its report, *A Crucible Moment: College Learning and Democracy's Future*—which was presented at the White House in 2012—the National Task Force on Civic Learning and Democratic Engagement highlighted several indicators of "Anemic US Civic Health." Among these are:

1. US ranked 139th in voter participation of 172 world democracies in 2007.
2. Only 10 percent of US citizens contacted a public official in 2009-10.
3. Only 24 percent of graduating high school seniors scored at the proficient or advanced level in civics in 2010, fewer than in 2006 or 1998.
4. Less than one-half of 12th graders reported studying international topics as part of a civic education.
5. Half of US states no longer require civics education for high school graduation.
6. Among 14,000 college seniors tested in 2006 and 2007, the average score on a civic literacy exam was just over 50 percent, an "F."[17]

These findings reveal that Americans' increasing ignorance about their country's foundational principles correlates with a greater disengagement from society. America's youth are failing to participate in the kinds of civic activities that formed the stuff of vigilance so admonished during the Founding era.[18]

The problem is not simply that young people are not reading the Constitution or that they are ambivalent about civics lessons. A larger problem is that young Americans are becoming increasingly ambivalent about education in general, and that a significant number of Americans—both young and old—are simply not reading. Several recent studies have concluded that twenty-first-century high school and college students care little about education and learning. Sociologists Richard Arum and Josipa Roksa write: "In a recent study, sociologist Mary Grigsby found that students widely embraced cultural scripts of college life depicted in popular movies such as *Animal House* (1978) and *National Lampoon's Van Wilder* (2002) that 'give the impression that a hedonistic collegiate culture is dominant.' These media depictions of college life provide students with normative frames of reference that define nonacademic collegiate behaviors and orientations as widely practiced, acceptable, and institutionally tolerated." Arum and Roksa also cite anthropologist Rebekah Nathan (a pseudonym), who, in her fifties, enrolled as a freshman in college in order to research twenty-first-century undergraduate culture. Nathan observed "how little intellectual life seemed to matter in college." In short, students today tend to prioritize social rather than academic pursuits.[19]

In the process, Americans are losing the skills and vocabulary they need to excel in nontechnical, nonmathematical fields. As one of our contributors, Mark Bauerlein, has argued elsewhere, "for students to earn good grades and test scores in history, English, civics, and other liberal arts, they need the vocabulary to handle them. They need to read their way into and through the subjects, which means that they need sufficient reading-comprehension skills to do so, especially vocabulary knowledge."[20] But if students today are not reading as much as they should be, then they are not developing these skills. And these reading skills are about more than just good grades and standardized test scores. Being able to read and write well is necessary for students to excel in their vocations.

Under the leadership of poet and former businessman Dana Gioia, the National Endowment for the Arts (NEA) undertook the enormous task of determining the state of reading in America today. "Most alarmingly," the NEA concluded, "both reading ability and the habit of regular reading have greatly declined among college graduates." This decline in reading has had "demonstrable social, economic, cultural, and civic implications" because nonreaders lose out on the numerous benefits of reading. "As with many other life skills," concluded one of the NEA's reports, "reading and writing fluency yield intangible benefits that sharpen the divide between those who have the skills and those who do not." Employees who are able to read and write well are more likely to receive higher financial compensation for their work and also to have more opportunities for career advancement. People who read literary works are also much more likely to visit art museums; to attend musicals, plays, and jazz or classical music concerts; to create works of art; to exercise, play sports, and enjoy the outdoors; and to vote. Americans who read regularly, according to the NEA, are also "more than twice as likely as non-readers to volunteer or do charity work." The study concluded that regular reading "seems to awaken a person's social and civic sense." Indeed, "Good readers make good citizens."[21] A sociological study of American soldiers in World War II similarly found that servicemen with higher levels of education performed better in combat, had higher personal expectations, thought more critically about problems in the military, had higher morale, were better at assessing difficult situations in a realistic manner, and were more likely to be promoted.[22]

The long-term and wide-ranging benefits of reading and being well-educated are beyond dispute. Better educated persons can generally expect to get more out of life. Thus, it is all the more disheartening that college students tend to be "motivated but directionless." For example, Arum and Roksa found that students choose courses in a way so as "to minimize short-term investments of individual commitment required to obtain high course marks." In other words, they tend to pick the "easy A" classes instead of the intellectually challenging ones. "Decisions are indeed based on personal preferences, but student perspectives are often exceedingly myopic and focused on short-term gains, understood as increased freedom from strenuous academic effort."[23] In a practical sense, then, students reinforce their own bad habits when they choose to take courses in which they will not have to read—or do much work—in order to pass. One self-perpetuating consequence of this trend is that students often do not perceive themselves as learning anything of substance or lasting value in their classes.

American society seems to cope with its own disturbing lack of education and civic knowledge by poking fun at the ignorance of ordinary Americans. One need only watch Jeff Foxworthy's *Are You Smarter Than a Fifth Grader* or Jay Leno's "Jaywalking" sketch on the *Tonight Show* to get a sense of the problem. Viewers in the audience and at home are usually astounded by the answers given to basic questions about America's history and form of government. But subdued beneath the laughter is the disturbing realization that these ordinary men, women, and children represent the future of American business, government, entertainment, and education. One wonders how long the republic can survive if current trends continue.

Lack of civic knowledge and ambivalence about the Constitution is not present only among television game show contestants and Jay Leno interviewees at Universal Studios. Not surprisingly, members of the intelligentsia routinely display ambivalence if not disdain for American constitutionalism. In December 2010, blogger and *Washington Post* staff writer Ezra Klein declared on MSNBC that the Constitution "has no binding power on anything" and that "the text is confusing because it was written more than a hundred years ago and what people believe it says differs from person to person and differs depending on what they want to get done."[24] Klein is certainly right that people disagree about the meaning of the Constitution. And without a dictionary by their side, most twenty-first-century Americans probably would not know what the clauses referring to bills of attainder or letters of marque and reprisal mean. But the problem is not that the Constitution is "more than a hundred years" old. The problem is that most Americans do not even attempt to know or understand what *their* constitution says or means, even though it *is* binding on their lives.[25]

Stepping into the void is a diverse group of educators, intellectuals and businesspeople, brought together in this volume, to grapple with the issue of civic illiteracy and its consequences. One of our contributors began his career as a scholar of the English romantic poet William Wordsworth; another as an intellectual historian of the American mind; two were businessmen (one of whom is also a poet); another is a historian of early modern English history; another had previously written about the poet Walt Whitman and early twentieth-century race riots in the U.S. South; one is a marketing professor; two study the Enlightenment; another is a former assistant secretary of state; and another began his career as an art historian of the Renaissance. But each of these authors has recognized the great need for what John Adams called "a frequent recurrence to the fundamental principles" on which the nation was founded in order "to preserve the advantages of liberty and to maintain a free government."

The purpose of this book is not to argue that all Americans must know and understand every facet of constitutional law or the American form of government. Nor is it that all Americans should enter an ivory tower in which they sit and dream about nothing but the life of the mind. Rather, as several of our contributors point out, Americans will be best served— and best prepared to live as good citizens of the nation—if they pursue a well-rounded, liberal education because a liberal education prepares a person to be free. An educated, informed, vigilant populace can help preserve the nation. As historian Merle Curti wrote in the midst of the McCarthy Era, "In a democracy blind, unthinking love of country must presumably give way more and more to intelligent and understanding patriotism, if that democracy as such is to survive."[26]

We recognize the challenges in delivering—and even defining—liberal or civic education given the current climate. Our contributors therefore present arguments attempting both to describe the state of American education and to scrutinize its goals. Their ultimate aim is to discover what liberal education, properly understood, entails. At times this volume uses the terms "liberal" and "civic" education interchangeably because it is difficult to conceive of the two separately within the context of a free republic. Government-funded education, such as that provided in the United States, inherently serves some civic purpose. Further, it may simply be the case that education cannot avoid teaching civic lessons whether or not it explicitly intends to do so.

This book is divided into three parts. The first section explores the history and philosophical foundations of the liberal arts tradition and its relation to civic education in a free republic. The section opens with an essay by E. D. Hirsch which traces the development of the content and teaching pedagogy of the American common school. In critiquing the child-centered approach that now dominates public education, Hirsch provides an argument for the civic necessity of the common school. Education ought not focus merely on skills, but must contain the type of content that enables meaningful citizen participation. He concludes that civic knowledge is prerequisite for general skills—and must be provided to all students. Next, Wilfred M. McClay argues that civic education has the express purpose of preserving the nation's memory so as to perpetuate the republic. Historical memory nurtures a fellow-feeling that connects the present generation to their forebears and thus enables Americans to recommit themselves to the nation's ideals. Finally, Andrea Radasanu's chapter reminds us of Montesquieu's defense of civic education to produce the kind of character required by healthy republics. Citizens of this particular form of government, Montesquieu urges, are particularly needful of civic education to moderate patriotism which might otherwise become overly ambitious or self-serving.

In order to be successful, educators must take into account the world in which young Americans live. The second section therefore explores three trends that are altering the nature of civic life in America: changing educational standards, the increasing role of technology in young Americans' lives, and the cutthroat marketing techniques employed in politics. First, Bruce Cole criticizes contemporary initiatives to eliminate important portions of American history from public education. Failure to teach actual historical content, he argues, threatens to undermine Americans' understanding of their nation's own founding creed. The ideas that bind the nation together can only be sustained by continual—and actual—study of America's foundational documents. Next, Mark Bauerlein points to technology as the leading force undermining the civic, social, and cultural skills of America's youth. The hyper-individualistic world of social media creates an anti-intellectual disposition that undermines the influence of adults and confines young adults to the narrowness of their peers. Today's enormous challenge for parents and educators is to prepare these young citizens for meaningful engagement in the world. Finally, Lisa Spiller and Jeff Bergner uncover the twenty-first-century version of what Madison called "the vicious arts by which elections are too often carried."[27] Uneducated, uninformed, or ambivalent voters make easy prey for the consumer-driven marketing techniques now becoming central to modern political campaigns. To combat these assaults, voters today must arm themselves with at least a minimal amount of civic knowledge.

Each of the foregoing trends highlights increasing challenges for today's educators and underscores the need to revisit our educational goals. Our final section therefore admonishes readers to consider what the goals of education in America ought to be. Jonathan Yonan argues that a liberal arts education should not be reduced to the "servile arts," that is, mere training in skill sets. Rather, the end goal is to educate and ennoble the human soul, which ultimately will prepare citizens to be free, rational, thinking individuals. Peter A. Benoliel, by contrast, argues that the liberal arts are desirable in their ability to prepare students for *both* vocation and life. In addition, Benoliel believes that a traditional liberal arts education needs to be supplemented with mandatory national service which would provide career training and, more importantly, civic consciousness among American youth. Finally, John Agresto points out the American tendency to see everything in practical terms, but he argues that utilitarian defenses of the liberal arts make us lose sight of what the liberal arts can truly do. When pursued for their own sake, the liberal arts help us understand the deepest longings of the human soul. Such profound insights can also be put to practical use, but they ought not be pursued merely for their practicality.

Lest we forget the "arts" in the "liberal arts," Dana Gioia's afterword reminds us of the centrality of the arts to civic education. The real purpose of arts education, he argues, is not to create artists or musicians but to cultivate complete human beings capable of living in a free society. As such, arts education is an essential—if not the central—educational component needed to heighten and beautify America's cultural, intellectual, and civic life.

In setting up the nation, John Adams wrote to his wife, Abigail, from Paris: "I could fill Volumes with Descriptions of Temples and Palaces, Paintings, Sculptures, Tapestry, Porcelaine, &c. &c. &c.—if I could have time. But I could not do this without neglecting my duty.—The Science of Government it is my Duty to study, more than all other Sciences." For Adams, at this formative period in American history, "the Art of Legislation and Administration and Negotiation" "indeed . . . exclude[d] in a manner all other Arts." He concluded: "I must study Politicks and War that my sons may have liberty to study Mathematicks and Philosophy. My sons ought to study Mathematicks and Philosophy, Geography, natural History, Naval Architecture, navigation, Commerce and Agriculture, in order to give their Children a right to study Painting, Poetry, Musick, Architecture, Statuary, Tapestry and Porcelaine."[28]

Adams did not envision that his sons would be ignorant of politics, and that his grandsons would know nothing of mathematics, commerce, or biology. Adams would have loathed the thought of his grandsons and their children leading bohemian lives free from the cares and concerns of reality. To the contrary, Adams hoped that knowledge and opportunity would be cumulative and ever-expansive. Yes, his generation would face peculiar hardships in setting up the government so that his sons and grandsons could pursue new avenues of life and prosperity and leisure. But his sons and grandsons could not neglect the responsibilities of life. In Adams's formulation, the second generation still knew the responsibilities of the first, and the third still knew the responsibilities of the first two; but each generation—building on the last—could continually broaden their horizons and their pursuits of happiness.

NOTES

1. Virginia Constitution (1776), Declaration of Rights, art. 15; Massachusetts Constitution (1780), Declaration of Rights, art. 18. This language—or similar language and ideas—was copied by other states. See also the constitutions of North Carolina (1776), art. 1, sec. 35; Vermont (1777), Declaration of Rights, art. 18; New Hampshire (1784), Declaration of Rights, art. 38; Illinois (1818), art. 8, sec. 18; Wisconsin (1848), art. 1, sec. 22; and Nebraska (1866), art. 1, sec. 24.

2. Alexander Keyssar, *The Right to Vote: The Contested History of Democracy in the United States* (New York: Basic Books, 2000), 3–76. New Jersey permitted women to vote until 1807, and Massachusetts, New Hampshire, New Jersey, New York and North Carolina permitted African American men to vote during the Revolutionary Era.

3. Declaration of Independence (1776).

4. Such a declaration, for Lincoln, would prove "a stumbling block to those who in after times might seek to turn a free people back into the hateful paths of despotism." The Founders "knew the proneness of prosperity to breed tyrants, and they meant when such should re-appear in this fair land and commence their vocation they should find left for them at least one hard nut to crack." Abraham Lincoln, "Speech at Springfield, Illinois," June 26, 1857, in Roy P. Basler, et al., eds., *The Collected Works of Abraham Lincoln*, 9 vols. (New Brunswick, NJ: Rutgers University Press, 1953–1955), 2:406.

5. Frederick Douglass, "What to the Slave Is the Fourth of July?" July 5, 1852, in William L. Andrews, ed., *The Oxford Frederick Douglass Reader* (New York: Oxford University Press, 1996), 127–29.

6. Critics of this view of the Constitution include abolitionist William Lloyd Garrison or law professor Mark A. Graber, author of *Dred Scott and the Problem of Constitutional Evil* (New York: Cambridge University Press, 2006).

7. James Madison, "Memorial and Remonstrance against Religious Assessments" (1785), in Gaillard Hunt, ed., *The Writings of James Madison*, 9 vols. (New York: G. P. Putnam's Sons, 1900–1910), 2:185–86.

8. *The State of the Constitution: What Americans Know*, a survey conducted by The Center for the Constitution at James Madison's Montpelier (released September 2010). In the survey, 14.9 percent of respondents claimed to have read "all" of the Constitution; 12.9 percent had read "most" of it; 32.9 percent had read a "fair amount"; 31.2 percent claimed to have read "some" of it; and 8.1 percent had read "none" of the Constitution.

9. See Intercollegiate Studies Institute, *Our Fading Heritage: Americans Fail a Basic Test on Their History and Institutions*, "Additional Findings," available online at www.americancivicliteracy.org/2008/additional_finding.html (accessed June 11, 2012).

10. Benjamin Franklin, "Proposals Relating to the Education of Youth in Pennsylvania" (1749), in Jared Sparks, ed., *The Works of Benjamin Franklin*, 10 vols. (Boston: Hilliard, Gray and Co., 1836–1840), 1:569–76.

11. George Washington, *Washington's Farewell Address, Delivered September 17th, 1796* (New York: D. Appleton, 1861), 16–17. Washington advocated for the creation of a national university in the nation's capital. For background, see Joseph J. Ellis, *Founding Brothers: The Revolutionary Generation* (New York: Alfred A. Knopf, 2000), ch. 4.

12. Thomas Jefferson, "A Bill for the More General Diffusion of Knowledge" (1779), in Paul Leicester Ford, ed., *The Writings of Thomas Jefferson*, 10 vols. (New York: G. P. Putnam's Sons, 1892–1899), 2:220–29.

13. Lincoln, "Address before the Young Men's Lyceum of Springfield, Illinois," January 27, 1838, in Basler, *Collected Works of Lincoln*, 1:114.

14. Lincoln, "Communication to the People of Sangamo County," March 9, 1832, in Basler, *Collected Works of Lincoln*, 8.

15. On the value of "Union" to nineteenth-century Americans, see Gary W. Gallagher, *The Union War* (Cambridge, MA: Harvard University Press, 2011).

16. Lincoln, "Address before the Young Men's Lyceum," in Gallagher, *The Union War*, 112. For graphic accounts of some of the violence to which Lincoln was responding, see David Grimsted, *American Mobbing, 1828–1861: Toward Civil War* (New York: Oxford University Press, 1998), 103–4; Daniel Walker Howe, *What Hath God Wrought: The Transformation of America, 1815–1848* (New York: Oxford University Press, 2007), 411–45.

17. See "Highlights from *A Crucible Moment: College Learning and Democracy's Future*," available online at www.aacu.org/civic_learning/crucible/documents/highlights.pdf (accessed June 6, 2012).

18. For an insightful analysis of the ways in which American institutions tend to promote selfishness over civic duty, see Quentin Kidd, *Civic Participation in America* (New York: Palgrave Macmillan, 2011).

19. Richard Arum and Josipa Roksa, *Academically Adrift: Limited Learning on College Campuses* (Chicago: University of Chicago Press, 2011), 81–82.

20. Mark Bauerlein, *The Dumbest Generation: How the Digital Age Stupefies Young Americans and Jeopardizes Our Future, or, Don't Trust Anyone under 30* (New York: Jeremy P. Tarcher, 2008), 126–27. On the bad effects of skimming, see Joseph T. Hallinan, *Why We Make Mistakes: How We Look Without Seeing, Forget Things in Seconds, and Are All Pretty Sure We Are Way Above Average* (New York: Broadway Books, 2009), 109–17.

21. *To Read or Not to Read: A Question of National Significance* (Washington, DC: National Endowment for the Humanities, 2007), 5, 77–91. In addressing the correlation between reading and civic participation and good citizenship, the NEA gives this caveat: "Although none of the data show cause and effect where reading and reader traits are concerned, the two reports do highlight several shared behavior patterns linked with positive individual, civic, and social outcomes" (86).

22. Samuel A. Stouffer, et al., *The American Soldier*, 2 vols. (Princeton: Princeton University Press, 1949), 2:36–37, 57–61, 121, 147–54, 245–59.

23. Arum and Roksa, *Academically Adrift*, 76.

24. In his blog, Klein later clarified that the Constitution is binding. See "Ezra Klein—Yes, the Constitution Is Binding," voices.washingtonpost.com/ezra-klein/2010/12/yes_the_constitution_is_bindin.html (accessed January 13, 2011).

25. The national survey by The Center for the Constitution at James Madison's Montpelier found that 66.1 percent of Americans believe the Constitution affects their lives "a lot" while 19.6 percent answered "some." See *Virginia Civic Health Index 2010* (Washington, DC: National Conference on Citizenship, 2010), 9.

26. Merle Curti, *The Roots of American Loyalty* (New York: Columbia University Press, 1946), vii.

27. James Madison, *The Federalist* No. 10.

28. John Adams to Abigail Adams, May 12, 1780, in Lyman Henry Butterfield, Marc Friedlaender, and Mary-Jo Kline, eds., *The Book of Abigail and John: Selected Letters of the Adams Family, 1762–1784* (Cambridge, MA: Harvard University Press, 1975), 260.

I

Foundations of Civic and Liberal Education

ONE

The Inspiring Idea of the Common School

E. D. Hirsch, Jr.

Since this country was founded it has been understood that teachers and schools were critical to the nation's future. In our own era, worried policy makers have fixed their eyes on our underperforming schools and devised new laws and free market schemes to make our students more competent participants in the global economy. There is understandable anxiety that our students are not being as well trained in reading, math, and science as their European and Asian counterparts. Reformers argue that these technical problems can be solved, and they point to exceptional islands of excellence among our public schools even in the midst of urban poverty. But the worries of our earlier thinkers about education would not have been allayed by such examples and arguments. The reason that our eighteenth-century Founders and their nineteenth-century successors believed schools were crucial to the American future was not only that the schools would make students *technically* competent. That aim was important, but their main worry was whether the Republic would survive at all.

It is hard for us to recapture that state of mind, but it is instructive to do so. The causes of our elders' concern have not suddenly disappeared with the emergence of American economic and military power. Our educational thinkers in the eighteenth and nineteenth centuries saw the schools as the central and main hope for the preservation of democratic ideals and the endurance of the nation as a republic. When Benjamin Franklin was leaving the Constitutional Convention of 1787, a lady asked him: "Well, Doctor, what have we got?" to which Franklin famously replied: "A Republic, madam, if you can keep it."

This anxious theme runs through the writings of all our earliest thinkers about American education. Thomas Jefferson, John Adams, James Madison, Franklin, and their colleagues consistently alluded to the fact that republics have been among the least stable forms of government and were always collapsing from their internal antagonisms and self-seeking citizens. The most famous example was the republic of ancient Rome, which was taken over by the unscrupulous Caesars and destroyed by what the American founders called "factions."[1] These were seen to be the chief danger we faced. Franklin and Benjamin Rush from Pennsylvania, Madison, Jefferson, and George Washington from Virginia, and their colleagues thought that a mortal danger lay in our internal conflicts—Germans against English, state against state, region against region, local interests against national interests, party against party, personal ambition against personal ambition, religion against religion, poor against rich, uneducated against educated. If uncontrolled, these hostile factions would subvert the common good, breed demagogues, and finally turn the Republic into a military dictatorship, just as in ancient Rome.

To keep that from happening, we would need far more than checks and balances in the structure of the national government. We would also need a special new brand of citizens who, unlike the citizens of Rome and other failed republics, would subordinate their local interests to the common good. Unless we created this new and better kind of modern personality we would not be able to preserve the Republic. In *The Federalist* No. 55, Madison conceded the danger and the problem: "As there is a degree of depravity in mankind which requires a certain degree of circumspection and distrust: So there are other qualities in human nature, which justify a certain portion of esteem and confidence. Republican government presupposes the existence of these qualities in a higher degree than any other form."[2]

Our early thinkers about education thought the only way we could create such virtuous, civic-minded citizens was through common schooling. The school would be the institution that would transform future citizens into loyal Americans. It would teach common knowledge, virtues, ideals, language, and commitments. Benjamin Rush, a signer of the Declaration of Independence, wrote one of the most important early essays on American education, advocating a common elementary curriculum for all. The paramount aim of the schools, he wrote, was to create "republican machines."[3] George Washington bequeathed a portion of his estate to education in order "to spr[ea]d systemactic ideas through all parts of this rising Empire, thereby to do away local attachments and State prejudices."[4] Thomas Jefferson's plan for the common school aimed to secure not only the peace and safety of the Republic but also social fairness and the best leaders. He outlined a system of elementary schooling that required all children, rich and poor, to go to the same school so that they would get an equal chance regardless of who their parents happened to be. Such notions about the civic necessity of the common school animated American thinkers far into the nineteenth century. In 1852 Massachusetts became the first state to make the common school compulsory for all children, and other states followed suit throughout the later nineteenth century. The idea of the common school dated back much earlier in Massachusetts, and in 1812 New York State passed the Common School Act, providing the basis for a statewide system of public elementary schools.[5]

By the phrase "common school" our early educational thinkers meant several things. Elementary schools were to be universal and egalitarian. All children were to attend the same school, with rich and poor studying in the same classrooms. The schools were to be supported by taxes and to have a common, statewide system of administration. And the early grades were to have a common core curriculum that would foster patriotism, solidarity, and civic peace as well as enable effective commerce, law, and politics in the public sphere.[6] The aim was to assimilate not just the many immigrants then pouring into the nation but also native-born Americans who came from different regions and social strata into the common American idea. Abraham Lincoln, who was to ask in his most famous speech whether any nation conceived in liberty and dedicated to equality could long endure, made the necessity of republican education the theme of a wonderful early speech, "The Perpetuation of Our Political Institutions," given in 1838, long before he became president. The speech echoes Madison and Franklin in stressing the precariousness of our republic. In order to sustain the Union, Lincoln said, parents, pastors, and schools must diligently teach the common American creed.[7]

It is illuminating to read the Lincolnesque speeches of the state education superintendents and governors of New York in the early and mid-nineteenth century. Like Madison and Lincoln, these New Yorkers understood that the American political experiment, which left everyone undisturbed in their private sphere, depended on a common public sphere that only the schools could create. New York State, with its diversity of immigrants and religious affiliations, was especially alert to the need to build up a shared domain where all these different groups could meet as equals on common ground. The speeches of the state's governors and superintendents are filled with cautionary references to the South American republics, which were quickly collapsing into military dictatorships. Unless our schools created Americans, they warned, that would be our fate. As Governor Silas Wright said in his address to the legislature in 1845:

> On the careful cultivation in our schools, of the minds of the young, the entire success or the absolute failure of the great experiment of self

government is wholly dependent; and unless that cultivation is increased, and made more effective than it has yet been, the conviction is solemnly impressed by the signs of the times, that the American Union, now the asylum of the oppressed and 'the home of the free,' will ere long share the melancholy fate of every former attempt of self government. That Union is and must be sustained by the moral and intellectual powers of the community, and every other power is wholly ineffectual. Physical force may generate hatred, fear and repulsion; but can never produce Union. The only salvation for the republic is to be sought for in our schools.[8]

As early as 1825, the New York legislature established a fund to secure common textbooks for all of the state's elementary schools, specifying that "the printing of large editions of such elementary works as the spelling book, an English dictionary, a grammar, a system of arithmetic, American history and biography, to be used in schools, and to be distributed gratuitously, or sold at cost." The aim, they said, was *not* to

> make our children and youth either partisans in politics, or sectarians in religion; but to give them education, intelligence, sound principles, good moral habits, and a free and independent spirit; in short, to make them American free men [and women] and American citizens, and to qualify them to judge and choose for themselves in matters of politics, religion and government. . . . [By such means] education will nourish most and the peace and harmony of society be best preserved.

Exactly the same sentiments animated the great writers of our earliest textbooks, including Noah Webster and William McGuffey. They aimed to achieve commonality of language and knowledge and a shared loyalty to the public good.[9]

Out of these sentiments emerged the idea of the American common school. The center of its emphasis was to be common knowledge, virtue, skill, and an allegiance to the larger community shared by all children no matter what their origin. Diverse localities could teach whatever local knowledge they deemed important, and accommodate themselves to the talents and interests of individual children; but every school was to be devoted to the larger community and the making of Americans. By the time Alexis de Tocqueville toured the United States in 1831 and wrote his great work, *Democracy in America*, this educational effort was bearing fruit. Tocqueville took special note of how much more loyal to the common good Americans were than his factious fellow Europeans.

> It cannot be doubted that in the United States the education of the people powerfully contributes to the maintenance of the democratic republic. That will always be so, in my view, wherever education to enlighten the mind is not separated from that responsible for teaching morality. . . . In the United States the general thrust of education is directed toward political life; in Europe its main aim is to fit men for private life. . . . I concluded that both in America and in Europe men are

liable to the same failings and exposed to the same evils as among ourselves. But upon examining the state of society more attentively, I speedily discovered that the Americans had made great and successful efforts to counteract these imperfections of human nature and to correct the natural defects of democracy.[10]

Today, every political poll indicates that most Americans believe the country is headed in the wrong direction—in many domains. Hoping to recover our roots, many have turned to the Founding Fathers for guidance. Unexpectedly, I find myself doing so as well. It has taken me many years in the vineyard of educational reform to understand how American education lost its bearings. To remain ignorant of that history is to remain trapped within it. What John Maynard Keynes said about economic policy applies equally to education: "Practical men who believe themselves to be quite exempt from any intellectual influence are usually the slaves of some defunct [theorist]."[11] We need to break out of the enveloping slogans that hold us in thrall.

THE PUBLIC SPHERE AND THE SCHOOL

On PBS's *NewsHour with Jim Lehrer* a young Muslim woman in a headscarf, aged sixteen or so, was being interviewed. She was speaking earnestly about the Muslim community in the United States, and she was making a lot of sense. What most engaged my attention, however, and still grips my memory was her manner. This girl sounded just like my sixteen-year-old granddaughter. Her intonations were the same, and the smart, smiling, good-natured substance of what she was saying sounded just like dear Cleo—her vocabulary larded with "awesome" and "fantastic" and other enthusiastic expressions of the current youth argot. I thought: this girl is wearing a headscarf, but she is American to the core. I also thought about the ongoing controversy in France, where the government has barred Muslim girls from wearing headscarves to school. I do not doubt that this American girl wore her headscarf to her public school, and I would be surprised if anybody made a big deal about it. Friends have explained to me why France—another democracy, created a little later than ours in the eighteenth century—is now making such a fuss about Muslim girls wearing headscarves to school. I understand their explanations, but I think that France has failed to learn important principles from its own philosophers and our brilliant American Founders. Our schools and our society may not be doing as well as they should, but they are still doing some things right.

But how deep did this Muslim teenager's sense of solidarity with other Americans run? In a pinch, would she be more loyal to her religion and ethnic group than to her country? We always hope that none of us will ever have to make such a choice. In the United States we almost never have to, thanks to the political genius of America's Founders, together with the accident that they lived at the height of the Enlightenment, when principles of toleration and church-and-state separation were at the forefront of advanced thought. How deeply did she understand and admire those ideas? How well had she been taught the underlying civic theory of live and let live that, in human history, has proved to be the most successful political idea yet devised to enable people of different tribes to live together in safety and harmony? My guess, based on consistent reports of our students' lack of civic knowledge, is that she had not been taught very well.[12]

A lack of knowledge, both civic and general, is the most significant deficit in most American students' education. For the most part, these students are bright, idealistic, well meaning, and good-natured. Many are working harder in school than their siblings did a decade ago. Yet most of them lack basic information that high school and college teachers once took for granted. One strong indication that the complaints of teachers are well founded is the long-term trend of the reading ability of twelfth graders, as documented by the National Assessment of Educational Progress (NAEP), "The Nation's Report Card." The trend line is a gentle downward slope.[13] This decline in reading ability necessarily entails a decline in general knowledge, because by the twelfth grade, general knowledge is the main factor determining a student's level of reading comprehension.

This correlation between background knowledge and language comprehension is the technical point from which nearly all of my work in educational reform started. To understand a piece of writing (including that on the Internet and in job-retraining manuals), you already have to know something about its subject matter. The implications of that insight from my research on language shook me out of my comfortable life as a conference-going literary theorist and into the culture wars. My research had led me to understand that reading and writing require unspoken background knowledge, silently assumed. I realized that if we want students to read and write well, we cannot take a laissez-faire attitude to the content of early schooling. In order to make competent readers and writers who possess the knowledge needed for communication, we would have to specify much of that content. Moreover, because the assumed knowledge required for reading and writing tends to be long lasting and intergenerational, much of that content would have to be traditional.

The 1980s and early 1990s were not the best years to be saying this. At the height of the multicultural movement, which aimed to change and broaden American life, few educators wanted to hear that school should be more, not less, traditional in the content it imparted. My scheme to foster equality of opportunity was identified as right-wing, whereas anti-traditional school reforms that were labeled left-wing had the unintended consequence of depressing equality of educational opportunity.[14] Left and right both need to adopt a nitty-gritty educational pragmatism that is based on science and the nature of reading and writing, and reach a broad, nonpartisan agreement about the democratic goals of schooling.

Fortunately, even in the late 1980s and early 1990s many educators accepted my argument that children need to be explicitly taught the knowledge silently assumed in reading and writing. Back in the 1970s, the field of psycholinguistics was just beginning to emphasize that the chief factor in the comprehension of language is relevant knowledge about the topic at hand. Those findings have since been replicated many times, in different ways and with varying constraints, both in the laboratory and in the classroom, and have held up robustly.[15] One early experiment used the following passage: "The procedure is actually quite simple. First you arrange the items in different groups. Of course one pile may be sufficient depending on how much else there is to do. If you have to go somewhere else due to lack of facilities, that is the next step; otherwise you are pretty well set." Subjects could not make sense of these sentences until they were given a title explaining the subject matter.[16] But you do not need an artificial example to make this point about the need of familiarity with a relevant "situation model" to understand language. Here's a naturally occurring example culled fresh from the online site of the British newspaper the *Guardian*:

> A trio of medium-pacers-two of them, Irfan Pathan, made man of the match for his five wickets. But this duo perished either side of lunch—the latter a little unfortunate to be adjudged leg-before—and with Andrew Symonds, too, being shown the dreaded finger off an inside edge, the inevitable beckoned, bar the pyrotechnics of Michael Clarke and the ninth wicket. Clarke clinically cut and drove to 10 fours in a 134-ball 81, before he stepped out to Kumble to present an easy stumping to Mahendra Singh Dhoni.[17]

Even if one knows a bit about cricket, this is at the dim edge of comprehensibility for most American readers.

Yet the words are familiar enough. Comprehension is not just a matter of knowing words. There is not a single word except maybe "leg-before" that I could not use effectively in a sentence. What makes the passage incomprehensible to me is my inability to construct what cognitive scientists call a "situation model." This is a highly generalized insight. It is hard to find an example where this premise does not hold. Comprehension depends on constructing a mental model that makes the elements fall into place and, equally important, enables the listener or reader to supply essential information that is not explicitly stated. In language use, there is always a great deal that is left unsaid and must be inferred. This means that communication depends on both sides, writer and reader, sharing a basis of *unspoken* knowledge. This large dimension of tacit knowledge is precisely what our students are *not* being adequately taught in our schools. Their knowledge deficit is the major reason their reading comprehension scores remain low.[18] Specific subject-matter knowledge over a broad range of domains is the key to language comprehension and to a broad ability to learn new things. It is the cornerstone of competence and adaptability in the modern world. A shortfall in conveying this enabling knowledge is a chief cause of our educational shortcomings—including our glaring failure to offer equal educational opportunity to all children.

In contemporary America, some fortunate youngsters are apprenticed to the knowledge assumptions of the standard American language from their earliest days because their educated parents and caregivers use that language at home. Other, disadvantaged youngsters are less familiar with the usage conventions and tacitly assumed knowledge of the standard language. Still others come from homes where parents are neither literate nor English-speaking. American schools need to help all of these students join the big-tented, all-accepting American public sphere by enabling them to become full members of the wider speech community with its tacitly assumed knowledge. An initiation into this public sphere does not require rejecting the private sphere that nurtured them.

Membership in this public sphere means mastery of the formal codes of speech and of the tacit knowledge that makes formal speech intelligible—shared information about football, civics, and so on. Some educators have wishfully asserted that our students will gain this shared knowledge through their pores by interacting with their peers and listening to tunes on iPods. The disastrously low and still declining performance on reading tests in the eighth and twelfth grades is decisive evidence that they do not gain this enabling knowledge, despite our schools' strong emphasis on reading under No Child Left Behind.[19] Indeed, the disappointing results of that law owe less to its defects than to flaws in the scientifically inadequate how-to theory of reading comprehension, on which so much time is being wasted in the schools to fulfill the law's provisions.

I am a political liberal, but once I recognized the relative inertness and stability of the shared background knowledge students need to master reading and writing, I was forced to become an educational conservative. The tacit, intergenerational knowledge required to understand the language of newspapers, lectures, the Internet, and books in the library is inherently traditional and slow to change. Logic compelled the conclusion that achieving the democratic goal of high universal literacy would require schools to practice a large measure of educational traditionalism. This insight has required a tolerance for paradox and complexity that, unfortunately, many have found impossible to accept. Their resistance has greatly slowed practical progress in American education.

The connection between liberal social ideals and conservative school practices was well grasped by the revolutionaries who founded

American education.[20] In eighteenth-century America, early schoolbook writers like Noah Webster understood the need not only to set forth the grammar, spelling, and vocabulary of the American standard language but also to teach the tacit knowledge, shared by everyone in the public sphere, which was taken for granted in speech and writing. Hugh Blair also had this idea of shared background knowledge in view when he published his *Lectures on Rhetoric and Belles Lettres* in 1783—informing both Britons and Americans what they needed to know (besides the English Bible) to communicate in the public sphere. His book went through printing after printing in the United States: I find 124 different editions of Blair's *Rhetoric* listed in the catalog of the Harvard University library—surely one of publishing's greatest successes! Between 1802 and 1812 Noah Webster produced his *Elements of Useful Knowledge*, covering some of the highly varied topics he thought all Americans should know.[21] Beginning in 1836, William McGuffey produced another American bestseller in his grade-by-grade series of *Eclectic Readers*. He called them "eclectic" because, like Blair and Webster, he knew that effective communication and intellectual competence require shared knowledge over a wide range of topics.

More is at stake in updating this tradition of publicly shared knowledge than just enabling our students to make higher scores on reading tests. Those scores do correlate with a student's ability to learn and to earn a good living,[22] but they also connect with something less tangible: a sense of belonging to a wider community and a feeling of solidarity with other Americans. When we become full members of the American speech community, we belong to a wider group toward which we feel a sense of loyalty. In large human collectivities, shared language and the accompanying shared knowledge are the chief agents of the sense of belonging. When people speak of "ethnicity," their meaning always includes the idea of a language community. Too often, ethnicity is thought of as something deeper than publicly shared language and knowledge—something quasi-racial. But school-based Hispanic ethnicity, say, is no more natural or innate than school-based American ethnicity. Standard written and spoken Spanish, with its eighteenth-century dictionary and its school-promulgated knowledge assumptions, was just as artificially constructed as Standard American English, which was formed with the help of Dr. Johnson's dictionary and schoolmasters like Blair, Webster, and McGuffey.[23]

Since language itself depends on shared knowledge and values as well as shared conventions, the aim of bringing children into the public speech community is a more than linguistic aim. All children need to be taught the general knowledge that is silently assumed in that language community. Our schools need to assimilate into the public sphere not just new immigrants but *all* of our children, regardless of family background. That is a fundamental aim of schooling in a democracy and one that we are not serving very effectively today. "Assimilation" sounds like a political or ideological goal, but it is also very much a technical necessity for effective education, because reading, writing, speaking, listening, teaching, and learning require the possession of the shared tacit knowledge of the language community.

Horace Mann understood that shared knowledge is essential to our sense of solidarity and harmonious well-being. Often called the "father of American public education," Mann explained this concept memorably in his twelfth annual report to the citizens of Massachusetts, in 1848:

> Property and labor in different classes are essentially antagonistic; but property and labor in the same class are essentially fraternal. . . . A fellow-feeling for one's class or caste is the common instinct of hearts not wholly sunk in selfish regards for person, or for family. The spread of education, by enlarging the cultivated class or caste, will open a wider area over which the social feelings will expand; and, if this education should be universal and complete, it would do more than all things else to obliterate factitious distinctions in society.[24]

My purpose is not to assert simply that the good done by Webster, McGuffey, and Mann was disastrously undone by the twentieth-century educators who overturned their principles. Though that is in fact the case, I will not hark back to a golden age that never existed. My aim is to rethink, from first principles, what our schools need to be doing now. We know more than any of our predecessors did about language and learning. We know more about the policies fostering high competence in the most successful national school systems elsewhere in the world. We know more about why our inner-city schools have been failing: not simply because of high poverty and family neglect but also because of content poverty and curricular incoherence. Compared to former eras, we have a far more capacious view of what makes up our multiethnic American identity. In sum, the new goals of our schooling do not depend on recapturing some idealized past. Such an aim would merely open an endless debate about the unfortunate way things really were during the WASPish days of Noah Webster and William McGuffey, whose schoolbooks served up significant doses of bigotry, pugnacious nationalism, and sectarian religiosity. The goals we need to set ourselves are those that promise a still better school tradition in the future.

THE COMMUNITY-CENTERED SCHOOL

Although the specifics of schooling in the twenty-first century must be new, the larger aim upon which American schooling needs to be founded is the same as in Webster's day—to develop the common public sphere in order to liberate and safeguard the heterogeneous private sphere. In the United States I can form any private association I choose and worship as I please. The chauvinistic Webster thought such freedom made America superior to the Europeans: "America founds her empire upon the idea of universal toleration: She admits all religions into her bosom—She secures the sacred rights of every individual; and (astonishing absurdity to Europeans!) she sees a thousand discordant opinions live in the strictest harmony."[25] To accomplish this feat of harmony, Webster thought we would need to create a common public sphere by means of the schools. His dictionary and schoolbooks were elements of his tireless efforts to create this public sphere.

Not just Webster but *all* of our earliest educational thinkers argued that precisely because we were a big, diverse country of immigrants, our schools should offer many common topics to bring us together; if schools did so, they felt, we would be able to communicate with one another, act as a unified republic, and form bonds of loyalty and patriotism among our citizens. In 1795, the members of the American Philosophical Society announced an essay competition on the subject of the best system of education "adapted to the genius of the United States." The prize was divided between two outstanding contestants, Samuel Knox and Samuel Smith, both of whose essays advocated a national core curriculum and, in Knox's words, "a uniform system of national education." Knox's co-winner proposed a national board of education that would set up and monitor this core curriculum.[26] The significance of this incident is not just that these two educational theorists independently advocated the idea of a nationwide core of commonality in education but also that their views found enthusiastic acceptance by the members of the society.

This idea of commonality in the early curriculum was far from a radical idea in 1797, when the American Philosophical Society published the prize essays. It was already the consensus view of such earlier writers as Jefferson and Rush. Benjamin Rush, in his 1786 essay "Thoughts upon the Mode of Education Proper in a Republic," was quite explicit about commonality. He reasoned that the extraordinary diversity of our national origins argued powerfully for a core of uniformity in our schooling:

> I conceive the education of our youth in this country to be peculiarly necessary in Pennsylvania while our citizens are composed of the natives of so many different kingdoms in Europe. Our schools of learning, by producing one general and uniform system of education, will render the mass of the people more homogeneous and thereby fit them more easily for uniform and peaceable government.[27]

The word "homogeneous" might horrify many who have been taught to honor individual differences. But these inaugural thinkers were not advocating what some might reflexively (and mistakenly) label "lockstep education." They were simply not focusing on the private dimension of schooling—the development of personal talent and individuality—an aim of *private* cultivation that they fully supported. Long before modern sociology they were focused on readying students for what sociologists now call the public sphere.[28] Many of their statements show that they were concerned with children's individual talents, and even with their private happiness, as well as their virtues. But their main emphasis was on the child's future public responsibilities as a citizen of the Republic.

Today, the idea of commonality is labeled un-American because it conflicts with our more capacious idea of American identity, which can no longer be described by the imperialistic metaphor of the melting pot but by the multicultural metaphor of the salad bowl. This is an oversimplification. Our early educational thinkers conceived of the United States as both a salad bowl and a melting pot—a federated union. Salad bowl and melting pot are not mutually exclusive concepts—and they cannot be if we are to have a bowl to hold the salad. The recent debates over multiculturalism have obscured the founding political conception of the United States, one of commonality with diversity, the *pluribus* within the *unum.*

Fundamental to this founding concept is the distinction between the public and private spheres of life.[29] The Founders expressed it with greatest clarity when speaking about religion, but this distinction was meant to apply very broadly in the American system.[30] We operate in the public sphere whenever we vote, serve in the military, transact business, become a member of a jury or a defendant at the jury's mercy, write for a big, unseen audience, or encounter any situation where we wish to be understood by strangers. This public sphere is the melting pot, where common laws, a common language, and shared unspoken knowledge and values are needed to make the uttered language comprehensible.

The private sphere is a more capacious realm, especially in tolerant America with its protections against intrusive government and its freedoms of association, speech, and action. That is the sphere of the salad bowl. It is neither literally private nor purely individual; our diverse and ever-changing systems of association are, on the contrary, highly social. Political philosopher John Rawls has called us "a social union of social unions."[31] "Private" associations are private only in the sense of being out of the reach of government and enjoyed peacefully apart from our legal, civic, and moral duties as members of the wider public community. Philosopher Richard Rorty offered the "club" and the "bazaar" as an alternative image for the public/private distinction—a lot of private clubs facing out on a big, open public bazaar. Yet another image is very New England—private houses and churches surrounding a public commons, a space where all can consort as equals. For those of us who advocate the common school, this latter has the advantage of using the word "commons."

The conviction that our schools need to make Americans out of all children, native or immigrant, was a sentiment that grew in strength in the nineteenth-century common-school movement. This is not to suggest that state control of schools and commonality of content was ever complete. Localities were always reluctant to pay taxes or cede full control.[32] But the common-school movement succeeded in establishing the conscious goal of preparing Americans for the public sphere and was thus an authentic extension of the founding ideas of Jefferson, Rush, and Webster.

The basic structural idea is still sound. In the early grades of schooling in a democracy, the public sphere *should* take priority. No matter what special talents and interests we may encourage in a young child, all of us have to learn the same base-ten system of arithmetic; the same twenty-six-letter alphabet; the same grammar, spelling, and connotations of words; and the same basic facts about the wider community to which we belong. Most modern nations impose that kind of compulsory early education because neither a democracy nor a modern economy can function properly without loyal and competent citizens able to communicate with one another.

Under this founding conception, the early curriculum can be viewed as a set of concentric circles. At the core are the knowledge and skills all citizens should have. Beyond that is the knowledge, such as state history, that the individual state wants children to possess. Beyond that may be the knowledge and values agreed on by the locality. And finally, beyond that, are the activities and studies that fulfill the needs, talents, and interests of the individual student. From the standpoint of the public good, what must be imparted most clearly and explicitly are the central core elements common to all citizens of the Republic. These need to be set forth specifically, grade by grade, so that one grade can build cumulatively on the prior one, allowing school time to be used effectively and putting all students in a given grade-level classroom on an equal footing. This idea of commonality in early schooling is fundamental to the educational ideas of Jefferson, Washington, Rush, Knox, Smith, and Mann. The community-centered common school is a conception that needs to be updated and reintroduced.

THE RETREAT FROM COMMONALITY

"The Retreat from Commonality" is the heading of part 3 of *Education in the United States*, by Robert Church and Michael Sedlak, covering the early twentieth century. In it the authors trace the decline of "the common school" and the common-school movement, now relegated in our educational histories to the eighteenth and nineteenth centuries. Why did this good idea fade?

There was nothing inevitable in the retreat from commonality. What happened was quite contingent. Shortly before the beginning of the twentieth century, with a ferocity fueled by nationalistic self-righteous-

ness, advocates of a rival set of ideas attacked the common-school tradition—and even the idea of tradition itself. The new theorists said, "We
are not like Europeans; we are not slaves of the past. We are a practical
(and better) people who look to the future. Our methods of education
must reflect that." Painting a bleak picture of the mindless rote learning
of common-school education, the enthusiastic reformers heralded the advent of "the child-centered school."

The idea that began to take hold in the American educational community thus completely inverted the concentric circles described above.[33]
Instead of placing at the center of emphasis and concern the knowledge
and skill that *all* citizens should possess, the new center was to be the
individual child and his or her interests, talents, and needs. From concrete projects and activities, the child would build up skill and knowledge in a natural, motivated way. Even when social efficiency and vocational schooling were considered the principal aim, as they were by some
of the new theorists, the focus would still be on the temperament of the
individual student.

Above all, the traditional academic curriculum was to be rejected.
Schooling would no longer be subject-centered but would instead be
child-centered. Though a lot of ink was expended on such innovations as
unbolting school seats from their orderly rows, the indispensable principle of the new approach was that specific subject matter was no longer to
be determined in advance. Curriculum topics would emerge instead
from concrete projects and from the interests of the child. Knowledge
would be acquired naturally and indirectly. The child's "growth" would
be constructed from within and be in accord with his or her temperament. Independent thinking would be encouraged, and passivity
avoided.

The new conception quickly became dominant: it was promulgated
with vigor in our teacher-training institutions by the 1920s and 1930s.
From the outset, the movement employed black-and-white polarizations,
asserting that it alone exhibited loving sympathy toward the child. It has
held to a partisan refusal to acknowledge that a subject-centered common
school might possibly be child-centered and loving in the *manner* of its
teaching.

One consequence of the child-centered idea was to make controversy
over the specific substance of the curriculum unnecessary. The choice of
content would be secondary, even trivial: any reasonable material would
fulfill the chief purpose of schooling, which would be to impart the generalized skills of reading, writing, figuring, and critical thinking. Even as
I write this chapter, this conception is well represented in a recent edition
of the *New York Times*, which contains numerous letters about education
in response to a piece on the twenty-fifth anniversary of the famous 1983
report on American education, *A Nation at Risk*. The very first letter, from

a teacher, ends: "High schools need to focus on critical thinking skills, not facts."

This succinctly summarizes the theory now taught in our schools of education—although *no* knowledgeable cognitive scientist agrees with it.[34] The how-to conception of schooling has been hugely attractive. It promised to solve technical and ideological difficulties at one blow without the need to mandate any controversial "top-down" curricular decisions. Today, it is just as powerfully ingrained in American education as the child-centered idea. Taken together, the child-centered idea and the how-to idea constitute the modern tradition of American education. Common to both is an antipathy to a set curriculum and "mere facts." Progressivism may have been the name the movement's proponents liked to use, but it could more accurately be called "the anti-curriculum movement."

The consequences of the anti-curriculum movement are apparent in the schoolbooks children are now compelled to use. A look at current language-arts textbooks reveals a stark contrast to Webster, McGuffey, and their descendants, not just in bulk and glitziness but in their lack of any guiding principles of shared knowledge.[35] As late as 1940, some common subject matter was still being consciously set forth in schoolbooks, but by the 1950s that was no longer true: commonality in the early grades had collapsed. After a long struggle, the new set of ideas had overmastered the earlier tradition of providing every child with shared knowledge and democratic values.

Not surprisingly, tacitly shared knowledge among Americans has waned. Moreover, the anti-curriculum, formal-skills approach has wasted enormous amounts of school time in endless, unproductive drills. The child-centered idea, which was intended to engage the child's interest, has led to an approach that, besides being unproductive, tends to bore children to distraction.[36] Cognitive science suggests that a content-indifferent approach to education *cannot* succeed;[37] and experience confirms that it has not. Starting in the 1960s, a decline in reading and writing skills of high school graduates began to be alarmingly apparent. Recently they have even declined somewhat further, despite the frantic emphasis on reading skills under No Child Left Behind. Scores on the verbal Scholastic Aptitude Test (SAT) declined from a peak in 1963 to a low point around 1990. Since then they have remained rather flat.

Some claim that this precipitous fall in SAT scores was due to an increase in the number of low-income students taking the SAT, but Christopher Jencks, who studies social policy at Harvard, has shown that the explanation is inadequate.[38] He observed that during the 1960s and 1970s, the state of Iowa, like every other, suffered a steep decline in verbal scores, yet Iowa was then 98 percent white and middle class. A sharp increase in the number of low-income test takers could not explain Iowa's decline in verbal skills. Looking at examples from textbooks,

Jencks showed that the chief cause was what happened in the country's schools in the 1950s, when the twelfth graders were going through school. The cause of the decline was not so much an influx of low-income students but an influx of educators trained in child-centered, anti-curriculum ideas, along with an influx of skills-oriented textbooks reflecting the anti-curriculum point of view.

By the 1980s, many people were alarmed by the declining scores. In 1981 the secretary of education convened a commission to report on the state of American education; the report was issued in 1983. Titled *A Nation at Risk*, the report contained this memorable comment: "If an unfriendly foreign power had attempted to impose on America the mediocre educational performance that exists today, we might well have viewed it as an act of war. As it stands, we have allowed this to happen to ourselves."

The main practical outcome was an agreement by all the states to set up definite academic standards for their schools—the state-standards movement. But the policy makers had not foreseen that those in charge of creating those standards would be guided by the very same child-centered, anti-set-content tradition that had brought on the crisis. Even the vague word "standards" encouraged evasion of content. Those who had presided over curricular fragmentation were now charged with creating the new standards. The result often looked like this:

> Students will comprehend, evaluate, and respond to works of literature and other kinds of writing which reflect their own cultures and developing viewpoints, as well as those of others. Students will demonstrate a willingness to use reading to continue to learn, to communicate, and to solve problems independently. Students will use prior knowledge to extend reading ability and comprehension. Use specific strategies such as making comparisons, predicting outcomes, drawing conclusions, identifying the main ideas, and understanding cause and effect to comprehend a variety of literary genres from diverse cultures and time periods.[39]

Such empty guidelines (this one is from Arkansas) offer no guidance at all. The phrases could be copied and pasted into any grade level, and in fact that is how many states' language arts guidelines are constructed. They are monuments to the continuing triumph of the anti-curriculum movement.

Fostering a core of commonality appeals to most Americans.[40] Polls say that when people on the street are asked whether it would be a good idea for the schools to build up knowledge cumulatively, with one year building systematically on the prior one, they generally say yes. And if they are asked, "Do you think a definite core curriculum is probably the only way schools can accomplish that goal?" the answer is a more reflective yes. "Would it be a good idea, considering the many low-income students who move from school to school, for there to be some commonality from one school to the next?" "Yes, definitely."[41] These common-sense ideas are so attractive to an unindoctrinated mind that one of the most pressing needs in American education is to understand why these practical goals—one might even call them necessities of good schooling—have been so difficult to institute.

The chief reason, as previously mentioned, is that beginning in the twentieth century a new set of ideas began to guide our schools, causing them by the 1930s to start losing their sense of urgent civic purpose. By the 1950s they no longer conceived their chief mission to create educated citizens who shared a sense of public commitment and community. Their main emphasis shifted to the individual student's personal development. It was as if the public school had decided to train students more for private than public life. This shift did not take place because teachers and schools had abandoned their sense of civic responsibility. Rather, twentieth-century Americans had become optimistic about America. They no longer worried that the very stability and peace of the Republic hinged on diffusing shared knowledge and preparing virtuous, loyal citizens who would subordinate private aims to the good of the whole. By the turn of the twentieth century, educators confidently believed that the public cohesion of the country was firm, and that schools should therefore concentrate on the growth and development of individual children by means of activities, without letting a lot of book learning get in the way. The needed knowledge would arise incidentally from immersion in concrete projects and "hands-on learning" rather than from deadly "rote memorization of mere facts."

In the 1930s, when the ideas began to take over, this new, anti-bookish method was said to exemplify the superiority of American openness to the future—though it originated in writers of the European Romantic movement of the eighteenth and nineteenth centuries: Jean-Jacques Rousseau, Johann Heinrich Pestalozzi, and Friedrich Froebel.[42] One distinguished American theologian of the 1930s, Reinhold Niebuhr, complained that educational thinkers of the early twentieth century, like other Americans of the time, exhibited a deficient sense of tragedy in their optimistic reliance on children's natural development.[43] Other early critics of the new educational ideas joined Niebuhr in criticizing an overly credulous faith in naturalistic and individualistic approaches to school learning. Overconfidence in the natural development of the individual, these critics argued, was at odds with effective schooling.[44]

We can now see that the child-centered approach to education is at odds with the Founders' and Lincoln's sense of the fragility of the American experiment, whose perpetuation depends on the eternal vigilance of its schools and teachers. By the 1930s, the individualistic, anti-subject-matter ideas of child-centered schooling already dominated our teacher-training institutions, although some education professors did

worry that the new emphasis on the individual child paid too little attention to the needs of society. One distinguished professor at Teachers College of Columbia University, George Counts, created a sensation in early
1932 at a meeting of the Progressive Education Association by telling his
audience that if the new kind of child-centered education "is to fulfill its
promise it must lose some of its easy optimism and prepare to deal more
fundamentally, realistically, and positively with the American social situation." The movement, he went on to say,

> has focused attention squarely upon the child; it has recognized the
> fundamental importance of the interest of the learner; it has defended
> the thesis that activity lies at the root of all true education; it has con-
> ceived learning in terms of life situations and growth of character; it
> has championed the rights of the child as a free personality. All of this
> is excellent; but in my judgment it is not enough. It constitutes too
> narrow a conception of the meaning of education. . . . The great weak-
> ness of Progressive Education lies in the fact that it has elaborated no
> theory of social welfare, unless it be that of anarchy or extreme individ-
> ualism.[45]

Counts's hearers were so impressed that they immediately revamped the
meeting agenda to discuss the social issues he raised. What happened
thereafter is instructive. Educators began insisting that the fulfillment of
the needs of the individual child *and* the fulfillment of the needs of society are inherently harmonious aims. All will be well, therefore, if the
schools fulfill the needs of the individual child.[46] Today, our schools
continue to yoke the two aims together in their mission statements—
without altering child-centered pedagogy and an emphasis on individual
differences.[47] In American public schools since the 1930s, child-centered
wine has been poured into ever-new terminological bottles—the "open
classroom" in the 1970s, "constructivism" and "critical thinking" in the
1980s, and "Individual Learning Plans" in the 1990s. Individualistic, anti-
set-curriculum ideas still persist even in the face of the stern provisions of
No Child Left Behind. The great school reform that is needed at present is
for a common coherent curriculum imparting shared knowledge in all
important subjects, including civics.

NOTES

This chapter is adapted from E. D. Hirsch, Jr., *The Making of Americans: Democracy and
Our Schools* (Yale University Press, 2009), with the permission of the publisher.
    1. See Gordon S. Wood, *The Radicalism of the American Revolution* (New York: Vin-
tage, 1993), esp. pp. 102–3.
    2. James Madison, *The Federalist* No. 55.
    3. Benjamin Rush, "Thoughts upon the Mode of Education Proper in a Republic,"
from *A Plan for the Establishment of Public Schools and the Diffusion of Knowledge in
Pennsylvania* . . . (Philadelphia: Thomas Dobson, 1786), reprinted in *Essays of Education*

in the Early Republic, ed. Frederick Rudolph (Cambridge, MA: Harvard University Press, 1965), 9–23.

4. From George Washington's last will and testament: "It has been my ardent wish to see a plan devised on a liberal scale, which would have a tendency to sprd systematic ideas through all parts of this rising Empire, thereby to do away local attachments and State prejudices, as far as the nature of things would, or indeed ought to admit, from our National Councils." Washington, The Will in *The Papers of George Washington, Retirement Series*, ed. W. W. Abbot, vol. 4: April–December 1799 (Charlottesville: University Press of Virginia, 1999), 477–92.

5. Andrew S. Draper, "The Origins and Development of the New York Common School System," appendix in Sidney Sherwood, *The University of the State of New York: History of Higher Education in the State of New York* (Washington, DC: Government Printing Office, 1900).

6. Carl F. Kaestle, *Pillars of the Republic: Common Schools and American Society, 1780–1860* (New York: Hill and Wang, 1983).

7. For a more complete analysis of this speech, see chapter 2 by Wilfred McClay.

8. Samuel S. Randall, *The Common School System in the State of New York . . .* (Troy, NY: Johnson and Davis, 1851), 58.

9. Randall, *The Common School System*, 26, 57.

10. Alexis de Tocqueville, *Democracy in America*, trans. Gerald E. Bevan (London: Penguin, 2003), 355, 356, 364.

11. "The ideas of economists and political philosophers, both when they are right and when they are wrong, are more powerful than is commonly understood. Indeed the world is ruled by little else. Practical men, who believe themselves to be quite exempt from any intellectual influence, are usually the slaves of some defunct economist." J. M. Keynes, *The General Theory of Employment, Interest and Money* (New York: Harcourt Brace, 1936), "Concluding Notes."

12. The most recent data can be found in Mark Bauerlein, *The Dumbest Generation: How the Digital Age Stupefies Young Americans and Jeopardizes Our Future; Or, Don't Trust Anyone Under 30* (New York: Jeremy P. Tarcher/Penguin, 2008).

13. See E. D. Hirsch, Jr., *The Making of Americans: Democracy and Our Schools* (New Haven: Yale University Press, 2009), 88.

14. I explain this paradox fully in *The Making of Americans*.

15. An excellent short account and up-to-date summary of the research can be found in Daniel T. Willingham, "How Knowledge Helps: It Speeds and Strengthens Reading Comprehension, Learning, and Thinking," *American Educator* (Spring 2006), available online at www.aft.org/pubs-reports/american_educator/issues/spring06/willingham.htm.

16. The title was "Washing Clothes." See J. D. Bransford and M. K. Johnson, "Contextual Prerequisites for Understanding: Some Investigations of Comprehension and Recall," *Journal of Verbal Learning and Verbal Behavior* 11 (1972): 717–26.

17. "Australia Brought Down to Earth," *Guardian* Online, January 20, 2008.

18. E. D. Hirsch, Jr., *The Knowledge Deficit* (New York: Houghton Mifflin, 2006).

19. See Hirsch, *The Making of Americans*, 110.

20. As well as their twentieth-century successors Gramsci, Bagley, and Kandel. See Hirsch, *The Making of Americans*, 37–38, 63.

21. Webster moves from the solar system to the "Geography of the Surface of the Globe, Oceans, Mountains, Rivers, etc."; "Of the Rivers in the United States, Lakes, Falls, etc."; "Of the First Peopling of America, and a Description of the Natives"; "Of the Discovery of Settling of America by Europeans"; "Of the Discovery and Settlement of North America"; "Of Indian Wars"; "Of Political Events"; "Of Military Events"; "Of Bills of Credit"; "Of Piracy in the American Seas"; "Of Diseases and Remarkable Events"; and "Of Controversies and Dissensions among the Colonies."

22. See Hirsch, *The Making of Americans*, 152.

23. The Royal Spanish Academy was founded in 1713, and the king of Spain, Philip V, approved its creation on October 3, 1714. Its purpose was to "fix the words and

terms of the Castilian language in their greatest propriety, elegance and purity." Its continually updated dictionary continues to be the basis of school instruction in Spanish.

24. Horace Mann, "12th Annual Report [1848]," in *The Republic and the School*, ed. Lawrence Cremin (New York: Teachers College Press, 1957), 79–112.

25. Joseph J. Ellis, *After the Revolution: Profiles of Early American Culture* (New York: W. W. Norton, 1979), 170.

26. I do not advocate a national curriculum imposed from Washington. See Hirsch, *The Making of Americans*.

27. Rush, "Thoughts upon the Mode of Education Proper in a Republic."

28. This is the English-language version of the term *Offentlichkeit* made current by the German philosopher Jürgen Habermas, whose concepts have been influential in recent sociology. Habermas, *Strukturwandel der Offentichkeit: Untersuchungen zu einer Kategorie der burgerlichen Gesellshaft* (Neuwied: Luchterhand, 1962).

29. See Jeff Weintraub and Krishan Kumar, eds., *Public and Private in Thought and Practice: Perspectives of a Grand Dichotomy* (Chicago: University of Chicago Press, 1997).

30. For more on religion, see *The Making of Americans*, chap. 3.

31. John Rawls, *A Theory of Justice*, rev. ed. (Cambridge, MA: Belknap Press of Harvard University Press, 1999), 462.

32. Kaestle, *Pillars of the Republic*.

33. A key figure is Col. Francis W. Parker, who at the end of the nineteenth and beginning of the twentieth centuries began introducing ideas into his schools from the Romantic tradition of Rousseau, Froebel, and Pestalozzi.

34. A good brief summary of cognitive science on this issue is D. Willingham, "Critical Thinking: Why Is It So Hard to Teach?" *American Educator* (Summer 2007): 9–19.

35. Ruth Miller Elson, *Guardians of Tradition: American Schoolbooks of the Nineteenth Century* (Lincoln: University of Nebraska Press, 1964).

36. See Linda Perlstein, *Tested: One American School Struggles to Make the Grade* (New York: H. Holt, 2007).

37. See Hirsch, *The Making of Americans*, appendix 2.

38. Christopher Jencks, "What's Behind the Drop in Test Scores?" *Working Papers for a New Society* 6 (July-August 1978): 29–41.

39. See   rison.k12.ar.us/Elementary/grade%205/literacy.pdf   and   www. coreknowledge.org/mimik/mimik_uploads/documents/480/CKFSequence_Rev.pdf (both accessed June 2, 2012).

40. See Steve Farkas and Jean Johnson with Ann Duffett and Joanna McHugh, *A Lot to Be Thankful For: What Parents Want Children to Learn About America* (Washington, DC: Public Agenda, 1998).

41. Jean Johnson and Ann Duffett, *Where We Are Now: Twelve Things You Need to Know about Public Opinion and Public Schools* (Washington, DC: Public Agenda, 2003).

42. See my earlier book *The Schools We Need: And Why We Don't Have Them* (New York: Doubleday, 1996), 71–79. I do not discuss John Dewey in *The Making of Americans*. He wrote so much over so long a period and not always consistently that debates over Dewey always become fruitless and distracting. To my mind, the most telling critique of Dewey's educational ideas are to be found in the final chapters of Richard Hofstadter, *Anti-Intellectualism in American Life* (New York: Vintage Books, 1963). Hofstadter notes that Dewey's views depend on a "pre-established harmony" between the natural development of the child and the good of society—a doubtful proposition in Hofstadter's opinion and mine. My term for this point of view is "providentialism." The ideas that count practically for our schools are the maxims and practices of teachers gained from their training in education schools. See *The Making of Americans*, ch. 2.

43. Reinhold Niebuhr, *Moral Man and Immoral Society: A Study in Ethics and Politics* (New York: Scribner, 1932).

44. These dissenters, chiefly William Bagley, Isaac Kandel, and Antonio Gramsci, are discussed in Hirsch, *The Making of Americans*, 37–38, 63.

45. George Counts, "Dare Progressive Education Be Progressive?" *Progressive Education* 9 (April 1932): 260.

46. Probably the best critique of this "pre-established harmony" between concrete activities, individual development, and the needs of society is to be found in Hofstadter, *Anti-Intellectualism in American Life*.

47. Here from the Bank Street School for Children in Manhattan is a typical mission statement, "We seek to strengthen not only individuals, but the community as well, including family, school, and the larger society in which adults and children, in all their diversity, interact and learn. We see in education the opportunity to build a better society." www.bnkst.edu/sfc/.

TWO

Memory and Sacrifice in the Formation of Civic Consciousness

Wilfred M. McClay

Almost all Americans agree that our collective knowledge of our own past is pathetically and dangerous thin. Why then has the reform of history education turned out to be such a painfully slow, seemingly intractable process? Why have we had so little success so far? And what can be done to accelerate the pace of reform? These are mysteries well worth unraveling. The observations that follow will not unravel them all, but they are intended to lead us into a more useful discussion of our nagging, exasperating problem, and to point toward a range of possible solutions.

Such issues would have been consequential at any time in the nation's history, as the founders of the American republic well understood. "If a nation expects to be ignorant and free in a state of civilization," wrote Thomas Jefferson in 1816, "it expects what never was and never will be."[1] Our system of government presumes an informed electorate. But these issues have been given a whole new level of urgency by the demands of the moment. Never in recent memory has a knowledge of the American past been more imperative, and more useful. The novelist John Dos Passos expressed the reasons very well: "In times of change and danger when there is a quicksand of fear under men's reasoning, a sense of continuity with generations gone before can stretch like a lifeline across the scary present."[2] This saying, which might in the past have sounded like a mere windy platitude to some of us, took on powerful and restorative force in the wake of terrorist attacks and the severe economic crises of the past decade.

Whenever any nation is faced with a deadly challenge to its institutions and its well-being, it must find a way to reach within, and draw upon its deepest sense of itself. This is especially true of a great democracy, which depends for its unity and morale upon a foundation of shared convictions, broadly diffused through the population. It helps a great deal to know, and remember, that others in our nation's past have faced great challenges and prevailed. Sometimes, with nations as with individuals, the very act of rising to the occasion—and seeing how others have done so—can awaken strengths that might otherwise have lain dormant, or never emerged at all. We hardly know what we are capable of doing— until we have to do it. Adversity concentrates the mind on essentials. It may even transform us.

The hard fact is that we haven't made any substantial progress in improving young people's knowledge of American history in the more than two decades since the publication of *A Nation at Risk*, which memorably compared the adverse effects of miseducation to the effects of an enemy invasion.[3] This lack of serious improvement is confirmed with depressing regularity by most quantitative measures, such as comparative test scores. But it is perhaps even more powerfully evident in the impressions that seasoned observers carry away from conversations with young people, of high school or college age. The historian David McCullough recently remarked that, in three decades of lecturing at colleges and universities, he has seen a steady decline in students' historical sense. "I don't think there's any question whatsoever," he has observed, "that the students in our institutions of higher learning have less grasp, less understanding, less knowledge of American history than ever before."[4]

I don't think anyone seriously doubts that this is the case. I might add, too, that not only do students lack historical knowledge, meaning a basic "cultural literacy" regarding the facts of the American story. They are even more lacking in what might be called "historical consciousness"—in an awareness that the past is real, that it profoundly shapes who we are, and where we stand today, and that it is a precious resource to be drawn upon, especially in times of trouble and uncertainty.

This is partly a failure of imagination, but it reflects even more basic failures. I won't rehearse the dismaying statistics arising out of study after study, indicating stagnation or decline on all levels. But I am still especially dismayed by the 2000 study commissioned by the American Council of Trustees and Alumni (ACTA), entitled *Losing America's Memory*, which showed such loss to have occurred not only among average students at average schools, but among graduates of Harvard, Williams, Pomona, Chicago, and similarly elite institutions, the top 55 such institutions in the land.[5] So few of our students, even at our top-ranked institutions, are absorbing the fundamentals of American history and government that it is now reasonable to wonder whether there will be anyone to pass such knowledge on to the next generation.

All of which suggests, not only that we are not doing enough, but that we are not yet doing the right *things* to turn the situation around. Something is fundamentally amiss. One could not help but be heartened by the immediate and alarmed response from a then-influential senator, the late Robert Byrd, to the ACTA report, which has resulted in the appropriation of large sums of money targeted at the revitalization of the teaching of American history.[6] Still, one would be justified in remaining skeptical, as I am, about the potential for such efforts, unless they proceed from fresh thinking and fresh premises. Lack of money is not the root of all evil in education, or anything else. As the ACTA reports have shown, it certainly isn't the problem at our lavishly endowed selective colleges.

So where to begin? Perhaps a better place would be in reflecting in a more sustained way on what it means to regard history as a form of *memory*. It's a very commonly employed metaphor—as in the title of the ACTA study—and for good reason. But we often use metaphors mindlessly, automatically, without thinking about what they may really mean. Sometimes they mean much more than we give them credit for.

The impulse to "do" history seems to be intrinsic to us as human beings. We are remembering and storymaking creatures. What we call "history" is merely the intensification of that basic human impulse. But the cultivation of it is essential to the perpetuation of civilized life. Historical consciousness is to civilized society what memory is to individual identity. Without memory, and the stories within which memories are suspended, we cannot say who or what we are. We cannot learn, use language, pass on knowledge, raise children, establish rules of conduct, engage in science, or even dwell in society.

Nor can we have a sense of the future as a time we know will come, because we remember that other tomorrows also have come. A culture without memory will necessarily be barbarous and easily tyrannized, even if it is technologically advanced, because the incessant drumbeat of daily events will drown out all our efforts to connect past, present, and future, and thereby understand the things that unfold in time, including the path of our own lives.

Memory, then, is a crucial source of continuity. As Ralph Waldo Emerson put it, memory is "the cement, the bitumen, the matrix in which the other faculties are embedded. . . . Without it, all of life and thought is an unrelated succession."[7] It need hardly be said that the same things can be said of history, as the chief form taken by *public* memory.

But something more needs to be said. We don't acquire a life-enhancing memory, or a lively historical consciousness, through the mere piling up of facts. It is not as if the more facts you retain, the better off you are. It might make you a better *Jeopardy* contestant, but that is about the extent of it.

Instead, memory is most powerful when it is purposeful, and *selective*. It requires a grid, a pattern of organization, a structure within which facts arrange themselves in a particular way, and thereby take on significance. Above all, it requires that we possess stories and narratives that link facts in ways that are both meaningful and truthful, and provide a principal of selection—a way of knowing what facts are worth attending to. That is how and why we remember the most *meaningful* things. Without such patterns, the facts are unremembered, or arrange themselves haphazardly—and the past takes on the dismal form captured so memorably by that great anti-historical philosopher of history, Henry Ford, who is said to have disparaged history as "one damned thing after another."

A compelling illustration of what I'm talking about is recounted in David Shenk's fine book *The Forgetting*, which is not only an extraordinarily luminous study of Alzheimer's disease, but a sustained meditation on the meaning of memory—and thereby, one might say, of history. Almost every theme in the book has some corresponding parallel meaning for students of history. But let me settle for one here, one that may offer us some insight into the "mystery of history" at present.

Shenk recounts the fascinating case study of a man whom psychologists call S. He was a Russian journalist who "remembered virtually every detail of sight and sound that he had come into contact with in his entire life." His freakish talent emerged when an editor reprimanded him for failing to take notes at a staff meeting—and S proceeded to repeat back to him every word that had been spoken in the meeting to that point. The editor sent S to the distinguished psychologist A.R. Luria, who subjected him to a battery of tests, and confirmed that it was true: there seemed to be no limit to the number of details S could recall. He could, for example, memorize lengthy tables of random numbers in an instant, and recall them perfectly for decades to come. It seemed that the man literally remembered *everything*.[8]

And yet, Shenk adds, "he understood almost nothing," because he could not "make meaning out of what he saw." When presented with tables of numbers placed in a deliberate and obvious pattern, such as a standard ordinal sequence (1, 2, 3, 4, 5, etc.), he couldn't make out the pattern. He couldn't understand poetry, couldn't understand the law, and couldn't even remember people's faces, because facial expressions are so changeable, and he lacked the ability to generalize those differences into a single stable identity. He was chronically disorganized and struck most observers as dim-witted. As Shenk concludes, "this astounding man, then, was not so much gifted with the ability to remember everything as he was cursed with the inability to forget detail and form more general impressions. He recorded only information, and was bereft of the essential ability to draw meaning out of events."[9] For him, life was indeed "one damned thing after another."

As this case illustrates, the healthy brain actually has few physical limits upon what information it can retain. Something else has to come into play. What makes for genuinely intelligent and insightful memory is not the mere capacity for massive retention, but a certain balance in the mental economy of remembering and forgetting. In other words, memory takes an active role in thinning out the mental trees so that forests can be discerned. It is selective by nature, and its selectivity is an essential tool in the mind's quest for rational order.

This selectivity is neatly reflected in the etymology of the ancient Greek word *logos*, sometimes translated as "account" or "argument," which derives from the verb *legein*, meaning "to select." To give a rational, coherent, useful, and true account of something, one has to select the details to be stressed, and leave the others out. We remember those things that fit a template of meaning, and point to a larger whole. We fail to retain the details that, like wandering orphans, have no connection to anything of abiding concern.

What might the practical implications of these observations be, for the teaching and study of American history? Let me suggest three, just for starters.

First, that the movement toward a greater emphasis upon *content* in historical instruction, while generally a good thing, needs to be augmented by a greater concern with the *form* in which this content appears. We may feel that we're doing a better job when we see to it that students are saddled with required textbooks that contain all the requisite names, dates, concepts, documents, and the like. But there is no reason to believe that they will remember anything from the experience—unless the books in question do what textbooks almost never do, and provide a compelling narrative context within which the factoids can begin to take on life.

Instruction in history would make a quantum leap forward if we simply banned the typical American textbook—with all its false omniscience and phony neutrality, its confused and jumbled narrative line, its shallow and derivative analysis, its endless sidebars and busy designs and overly clever graphics, and its anxious bows in the direction of state textbook committees and various forms of political correctness, left and right. In its place, students should read real books, by real authors, with a real point of view, a winning writing style, and a story to tell. Such books do a far better job of stimulating the imagination. And they embody the selectivity that is essential to the formation of durable memory. If we want for our kids to cherish American history, that is what we need to give them.

Second, that the notion that we can finesse the disagreements in our culture by "teaching the conflicts" is based on a false, or at least very partial, understanding of what makes for historical knowledge and consciousness.[10] My own experience with such techniques has been decidedly mixed. Many students are so poorly grounded in the fundamental story of American history that they lack the ability to debate in an intelligent and informed manner. In addition, they are inclined to yawn at scholarly disputes, and conclude that, when even the experts cannot agree, there is nothing here worth their trouble.[11]

It is far better, and more responsible, to teach the American story in as straight a manner as possible, give students a strong underlying sense of their heritage—and then let them generate dissents and debates in response to it. Let me be clear that I am not advocating teaching American history as a myth or a whitewash. But to present American history as something highly problematic, and fundamentally conflicted and contested on every conceivable point—the default position of today's scholarship—is not only unilluminating as history but completely ineffectual as pedagogy. This is a fact that needs to be faced.

Third, that the design of our courses and our curricula is, and must be, an exercise in *triage*—in making hard choices about what gets thrown *out* of the story, so that the essentials can survive. The tendency in recent years has been almost entirely in the opposite direction, when the buzzword has been "inclusion." That is a good word, but we have applied it wrongly. It is always easy to include something new, to add another sidebar to the textbook account. But the result has been an increasingly incoherent story, or no story at all. The last thing we need is to emulate the mind of S, whose memory was nothing if not inclusive. Instead, we need to be willing to identify those things every American student needs to know, and insist upon them—an understanding of the origins and structure of the U.S. Constitution, for example—while paring away vigorously at the rest. Needless to say, this is almost as difficult as cutting the national budget, and for many of the same reasons.

What all three of these suggestions have in common is a renewed emphasis upon telling the American story in a clearer and more compelling way, with the selectivity that is imposed by the requirements of strong narrative. This is the right way to proceed, on its merits. But it may also have the virtue of fitting the public mood. Americans do not want to view the nation's history as merely a grab-bag of factoids. Nor, I think, are they going to find much sustenance in the relentlessly critical approach to American history so beloved of academic historians. Make no mistake, we need such critical perspectives, especially to protect ourselves against the human propensity for willful and self-serving illusion. They are necessary—but they are not sufficient. The more fundamental need—and the chief area in which we are failing so conspicuously—is the desire to establish a sense of connection with the past as something from which we can draw meaning and sustenance, something in which our own identity is deeply embedded. We need knowledge that will hold up in a foxhole. That image should suggest how critical a role the writing and teaching of history can play in the nation's intellectual and moral life.

It is not wrong, then, to say that the study of history needs to make itself useful in the present, and we shouldn't be embarrassed to say so. But in doing so, we need to think of "use" in a much broader way than we're accustomed to doing. Part of history's "use" is the way it lets us escape from the iron grip of the present, and gives proper weight to the dignity of memory and the reality of the past. That is admittedly a hard sell to young people—or to Americans of any age. We are a practical-minded and present-minded people. But that is precisely why historians should not forget, in the pressure to find practical justifications for what they do as historians, that they further an important public purpose simply by being what they are, and by preserving and furthering a longer, broader, and deeper kind of consciousness—a quality of mind and soul that a culture of ceaseless novelty and instant erasure has all but declared war upon.

I think there may be particular value in our revisiting Ernest Renan's celebrated 1882 essay "What Is a Nation?" (Or "Qu'est-ce qu'une nation?"), which defined a nation as an entity sustained by its historical consciousness. It is important to remember how different such a conception was from the alternatives on offer in late nineteenth-century Europe. For Renan a nation was fundamentally "a soul, a spiritual principle," constituted not only by "present-day consent" but also by the residuum of the past, "the possession in common of a rich legacy of memories" which form in the citizen "the will to perpetuate the value of the heritage that one has received in an undivided form." Permit me to quote from Renan at greater length:

> The nation, like the individual, is the culmination of a long past of endeavours, sacrifice, and devotion. Of all cults, that of the ancestors is the most legitimate, for the ancestors have made us what we are. A heroic past, great men, glory (by which I understand genuine glory), this is the social capital upon which one bases a national idea. To have common glories in the past and to have a common will in the present, to have performed great deeds together, to wish to perform still more—these are the essential conditions for being a people. . . . A nation is therefore a large-scale solidarity, constituted by the feeling of the sacrifices that one has made in the past and of those that one is prepared to make in the future.[12]

Renan strongly opposed the then-fashionable view that nations should be understood as entities united by racial or linguistic or geographical or religious or material factors. None of those factors were sufficient to account for the emergence of this "spiritual principle." Active consent had to be a part of it. But it was insufficient without the presence of the past—the past in which that consent was embedded, and through which it found meaning.

I think this account of the nation provides valuable insight for us. The ballast of the past, and of our intimate connection to it, is similarly indispensable to the sense of American national identity. It forms a strain in our identity that is in some respects far less articulate (and less frequently articulated) than the universalistic principles that writers like Walter Berns have emphasized, precisely because it seems to conflict with American assertions of universalism, and its intellectual basis is less well-defined. But it is every bit as powerful, if not more so, and just as indispensable. And it is a very particular force. Our nation's particular triumphs, sacrifices, and sufferings—and our memories of those things—draw and hold us together, precisely because they are the sacrifices and sufferings, not of all humanity, but of us in particular.

Fortunately, one does not have to rely exclusively on a French writer for such insights. No one has spoken of American national identity with greater mastery than Abraham Lincoln, and his words still endure. In his 1838 speech on "The Perpetuation of Our Political Institutions," delivered to the Young Men's Lyceum of Springfield, Illinois, Lincoln responded to the then-raging violence directed at blacks and abolitionists in Southern and border states, with an admonition that could have come from Toynbee: "If destruction be our lot, we must ourselves be its author and finisher. As a nation of freemen, we must live through all time, or die by suicide." The danger he most feared was that rampant lawlessness would dissolve the "attachment of the People" to their government. And the answer he provides to this danger is remarkable for the way it touches on the same themes that Renan recounts:

> Let every American, every lover of liberty, every well wisher to his posterity, swear by the blood of the Revolution, never to violate in the least particular, the laws of the country; and never to tolerate their violation by others. As the patriots of seventy-six did to the support of the Declaration of Independence, so to the support of the Constitution and Laws, let every American pledge his life, his property, and his sacred honor;—let every man remember that to violate the law, is to trample on the blood of his father, and to tear the character of his own, and his children's liberty. Let reverence for the laws, be breathed by every American mother, to the lisping babe, that prattles on her lap—let it be taught in schools, in seminaries, and in colleges;—let it be written in Primmers, spelling books, and in Almanacs;—let it be preached from the pulpit, proclaimed in legislative halls, and enforced in courts of justice. And, in short, let it become the *political religion* of the nation; and let the old and the young, the rich and the poor, the

grave and the gay, of all sexes and tongues, and colors and conditions, sacrifice unceasingly upon its altars.[13]

The excerpt shows Lincoln's remarkable ability to intertwine the past and the present, and evoke a sense of connection between them. The speech performs the classic republican move, back to the founding origins, connecting the public order explicitly with something so primal as a son's love of, and respect for, his father. Obedience to the law and reverence for the Constitution—these are directly connected with memory, the reverence owed to the sufferings of the patriot generation, and the blood of one's own father. Such words gesture toward his even more famous invocation of "the mystic chords of memory" in his First Inaugural Address, chords "stretching from every battlefield and patriot grave to every living heart and hearthstone all over this broad land," chords that provide the music of the Union.[14] He performs a similar move of memorial linkage in the Gettysburg Address, beginning with the Founding "fathers" and ending in a rededication and recommitment, drawn from knowledge of the "honored dead" who hallowed the very ground with their sacrifice.[15]

Lincoln understood that memories fade—even the memories of honored dead. The danger was that as America's collective memory of the Revolution diminished, so too would the American people's appreciation for the political system that they had inherited from the Founders. "I do not mean to say, that the scenes of the revolution *are now* or *ever will be* entirely forgotten," stated Lincoln, "but that like every thing else, they must fade upon the memory of the world, and grow more and more dim by the lapse of time." At one time, every American family had known a soldier who had suffered in the Revolution:

> The consequence was, that of those scenes, in the form of a husband, a father, a son or a brother, a *living history was* to be found in every family—a history bearing the indubitable testimonies of its own authenticity, in the limbs mangled, in the scars of wounds received, in the midst of the very scenes related—a history, too, that could be read and understood alike by all, the wise and the ignorant, the learned and the unlearned. But *those* historians are gone. They *can* be read no more forever. They *were* a fortress of strength; but, what invading foeman could *never* do, the silent artillery of time *has done*; the leveling of its walls. They are gone.[16]

These pieces of living history—these men who had fought in the Revolution—"*were* the pillars of the temple of liberty," Lincoln continued. But they had crumbled away. And now, according to Lincoln, "that temple must fall, unless we, their descendants, supply in their places . . . other pillars hewn from the solid quarry of sober reason." The people, in other words, must exhibit "*general intelligence, sound morality* and in particular, *a reverence for the constitution and laws*," in order for their nation to survive and flourish.[17] Preservation of the nation, for Lincoln, required the people to remember and appreciate and revere the sacrifices of their forebears.

John Adams himself had something exemplary to say about all this, and I would like to conclude with his words. Unlike his rival Thomas Jefferson, Adams composed no epitaph for himself in anticipation of his death. Yet Adams did compose an inscription for the sarcophagus lid of his ancestor Henry Adams, the first Massachusetts Adams, who had arrived in 1638, nearly a century before John's birth. The inscription, with which David McCullough concludes his biography of Adams, speaks volumes about how Adams conceived his place in history, and how he accepted the obligation to instruct the future by honoring the past:

> This stone and several others have been placed in this yard by a great, great, grandson from a veneration of the piety, humility, simplicity, prudence, frugality, industry and perseverance of his ancestors in hopes of recommending an affirmation of their virtues to their posterity.[18]

There is a philosophy of history, of sorts, embedded in these words. Adams was no fool about the faults and perversities of human nature. He was under no illusion that his forebears were perfect. But neither was he under the illusion that he, or his descendants, could live full and admirable lives without drawing on the resources those forebears had labored to create.

We have done well in addressing the first illusion. But in doing so, we have fallen into the arms of the second. Now may be the time to acknowledge that problem. It is a mistake to live without criticism of the past. But it is also a mistake to live without gratitude to it. The fullness of our humanity demands that we do both.

NOTES

Copyright is retained by the author.

1. Thomas Jefferson to Col. Charles Yancey, January 6, 1816, in Paul Leicester Ford, ed., *The Writings of Thomas Jefferson*, 10 vols. (New York: G. P. Putnam's Sons, 1892–1899), 10:4.

2. John Dos Passos, *The Ground We Stand On: Some Examples from the History of a Political Creed* (New York: Harcourt, Brace and Company, 1941), 2.

3. U.S. National Commission on Excellence in Education, *A Nation at Risk* (Cambridge, MA: U.S. Research, 1984).

4. Interview with David McCullough, in Bruce Cole, *Fearless and Free: Celebrating the 40th Anniversary of the National Endowment for the Humanities* (Washington, DC: National Endowment for the Humanities, 2005), 9.

5. Anne D. Neal and Jerry L. Martin, *Losing America's Memory: Historical Illiteracy in the 21st Century* (Washington, DC: American Council of Trustees and Alumni, 2000).

6. Miriam E. Hauss, "Senator Byrd to Receive the AHA's Theodore Roosevelt-Woodrow Wilson Award for Civil Service," *Perspectives on History: The Newsmagazine*

of the American Historical Association 41 (December 2003), available online at www. historians.org/perspectives/issues/2003/0312/0312new2.cfm (accessed June 22, 2012).

7. Ralph Waldo Emerson, *The Complete Works of Ralph Waldo Emerson: Natural History of Intellect and Other Papers* (New York: Houghton, Mifflin, 1893), 90.

8. David Shenk, *The Forgetting: Alzheimer's: Portrait of an Epidemic* (New York: Doubleday, 2003), 57–60; also in David Shenk, *The Genius in All of Us* (New York: Doubleday, 2010), 191–93.

9. Shenk, *The Genius in All of Us*, 191–93.

10. For an argument in favor of "teaching the conflicts," see Gerald Graff, *Beyond the Culture Wars: How Teaching the Conflicts Can Revitalize American Education* (New York: W.W. Norton, 1992); see also the Symposium on Graff's book in *Pedagogy* 3 (Spring 2003): 245–73.

11. For historian Joseph J. Ellis's take on the disconnect between professional historians and the general public, see *Founding Brothers: The Revolutionary Generation* (New York: Alfred A. Knopf, 2000), 12–13.

12. Ernest Renan, "What Is a Nation?" in Geoff Eley and Ronald Grigor Suny, eds., *Becoming National: A Reader* (New York: Oxford University Press, 1996), 52–54.

13. Abraham Lincoln, "Address before the Young Men's Lyceum of Springfield, Illinois," January 27, 1838, in Roy P. Basler et al., eds., *The Collected Works of Abraham Lincoln*, 9 vols. (New Brunswick, NJ: Rutgers University Press, 1953–1955), 1:112.

14. Lincoln, "First Inaugural Address—Final Text," March 4, 1861, in Basler et al., *The Collected Works*, 4:271.

15. Lincoln, "Address Delivered at the Dedication of the Cemetery at Gettysburg," November 19, 1863, in Basler et al., *The Collected Works*, 7:23.

16. Lincoln, "Address before the Young Men's Lyceum," in Basler et al., *The Collected Works*, 1:115.

17. Lincoln, "Address before the Young Men's Lyceum," in Basler et al., *The Collected Works*, 1:115.

18. David McCullough, *John Adams* (New York: Simon and Schuster, 2001), 649.

THREE

Polishing Barbarous Mores

Montesquieu on Liberalism and Civic Education

Andrea Radasanu

Most informed observers would agree that America suffers from low civic engagement, and that it is important to overcome this civic deficit by instilling norms of democratic citizenship in future generations of Americans.[1] Yet there is little agreement on what it means to foster norms of democratic citizenship, or, to use a more old-fashioned formulation, to imprint the duties of citizenship on the hearts and minds of citizens. This lack of consensus is perhaps to be expected given that America was founded on the premise that each individual citizen would be able to pursue his own understanding of happiness. The public or political sphere was secondary to the private one, in which individual opinion was king.

A generation after the Founding, Alexis de Tocqueville noted that Americans, natural Cartesians that they are, like to rely on their own reason and eschew all manner of tradition and history, which had been cornerstones of the collective life of past civilizations.[2] It is no surprise, then, that civic education today mostly means teaching citizens how to be tolerant, civil, and respectful of one another.[3] These qualities undergird procedural democracy in the context of a wide divergence of beliefs and priorities. Such virtues or values have little to say, however, about the common political project that we embark on together.

The conservative solution to the withdrawal into private life or "individualism," as Tocqueville called the democratic retreat into private concerns, usually involves an education in the Founding Fathers' intentions and the venerable institutions that have served American liberty. But this does not simply solve the problem, as the Founders were themselves unclear on the means of perpetuating the American republic. John Adams declared that the United States of America was the first example of a government "erected on the simple principles of nature."[4] Reflecting the Enlightenment faith in rationalism, the framers of the Constitution made no provision for civic education. Yet the Founders surely did suggest that the common project of America had inherent dignity, and was not merely a compact that allowed each individual to make his fortune unhampered by oppressive public morality. And they also readily admitted that this project's success depended on sacrifice, courage, and camaraderie, as opposed to being the result of individuals consulting their private interests. The Founders, after all, greatly admired the classical republican tradition.[5]

There is a tension between America viewed as a self-perpetuating regime that provides the framework for individuals to pursue their rational interest, on the one hand, and as a republic that represents a dignified common good and demands great sacrifices from its citizens, on the other. I suggest that there is no better thinker to help explore this tension than Montesquieu. Known as the "celebrated Montesquieu," he was probably the most influential philosophical figure at the Founding.[6] He inspired both the Federalists and the Anti-Federalists in the debate regarding the importance of virtue in republican government. The Anti-Federalists took up Montesquieu's "small republic thesis," which held that self-government requires virtue, which, in turn, requires a small territory and homogeneous mores. By contrast, the Federalists looked to Montesquieu's argument in favor of the new English commercial republican model, which depended not on virtue but on a law-abiding and domesticated desire for personal security and prosperity. This latter model could accommodate passionate disagreement and well-channeled ambition among individuals.[7]

In the end, the Federalists understood Montesquieu better than the Anti-Federalists. While Montesquieu writes that ancient republics depended on virtue and required a small territory, as Alexander Hamilton correctly notes, Montesquieu's solution to the security woes of small ancient republics points toward large, strong, and mostly centralized governments.[8] Montesquieu bequeathed to America the model of the English commercial republic, which had to recommend it the political liberty of individuals. This regime kept citizens safe from one another and from the encroachment of governmental authority on their private lives and beliefs. All of these great accomplishments were achieved, at least seemingly, without virtue and without public-spirited citizens. Montesquieu presents eighteenth-century Englishmen as anti-social, selfish, and not given to careful deliberation over matters of common concern. He declares them princes of their own fiefdoms, thus suggesting that civic virtue is simply unnecessary for sustaining liberty.[9] Yet Montesquieu is also very sensitive to ways in which physical and moral environments shape our natures, and denies that it is possible to enjoy a political regime in which liberty reigns without having and maintaining the disposition to be free. This implies that a certain kind of education is necessary to maintain our freedom even in liberal regimes that are organized around a proper understanding of human nature and fundamental human needs.

This chapter, then, investigates Montesquieu's account of the kind of education that is a prerequisite for and consistent with a liberal regime. First, I consider his general teaching on education in the various regime types he identifies. What emerges is a clarification of the differences between traditional civic education in the service of developing a sense of public duty, and education as it pertains to the new liberal commercial regime. Next, I go on to tease out specific Montesquieuian lessons on the education necessary to maintain political coherence in liberal states. Finally, I reflect on whether Montesquieu adequately dispenses with the tension between civic education and liberal politics, and the implications of any continuing friction between the two.

EDUCATION, CIVIC EDUCATION, AND POLISHING BARBAROUS MORES

In his early epistolary novel the *Persian Letters* (1721), a popular work that helped launch the French Enlightenment, Montesquieu throws down the gauntlet against the tradition of learning in the West. Rica, one of two Persian characters who visit the West in this novel, writes about his experiences in a large library housed in a monastery.[10] As Montesquieu suggests here, religious orders had control over education in eighteenth-century France, despite the fact that the French Enlightenment was on the rise and the French Revolution just around the corner. At first, Rica encounters the ranking monk of the order, who claims ignorance regarding the contents of the library. The ranking monk recommends the services of the librarian monk (useless to the order in all other ways, according to his superior) as a tour guide for Rica. This is fortuitous for Rica, as the librarian monk is affable, witty, knowledgeable, and generous. This enlightened monk and library guide teaches Rica to disdain much of the book collection, especially those books having to do with scholasticism and mysticism. Philosophy, which is presented as equal parts metaphysics, alchemy, and astrology, is also maligned.

Young Rica's guide has better things to say about the histories than about the other genres stored in the library.[11] Histories are informative and speak to human and political concerns. In particular, he says, they expose the abuses of the Church and Papacy, and provide a view of past and present, of liberty gained and liberty lost. Through this vignette and others, Montesquieu intimates that under the absolute monarchy of eighteenth-century France political histories offered a means to resist the universalizing tendencies of the Church, and a counterpoint to providential history. In reading these histories, one gains insights that challenge the authority of the Church to act as gatekeeper to all Western knowledge. Rica learns, for instance, that monkish learnedness and its co-option of ancient and medieval philosophy are not responsible for Western civilization. Rica also learns to prefer the barbarians who conquered Rome to the Roman civilization that succumbed to them. According to the enlightened monk, freedom first arose in the forests of Germany, and matured into English liberty.[12] The barbarians "were not truly barbarous since they were free." They became barbarous much later as they "submitted for the most part to absolute power" and so "lost the gentle (*douce*) liberty that conforms to reason, humanity and nature."[13] These rough people were unencumbered by superstition, and, although primitive and belligerent, knew and loved their freedom and independence. Taming the wild expression of their liberty, rather than teaching them notions of duty and obligation to the commons, is the education the Germanic forbearers of England required. Montesquieu, through this "useless" (*bon à rien*)[14] monk but very useful library guide, suggests that unlearning the habits and mores of despotism is as important or more important than learning those of liberty.

In his own name in *The Spirit of Laws*, Montesquieu goes on to assert the view that laws must be tailor-made for individual peoples.[15] His emphasis on particular histories that denote specific political arrangements and their implications for the life, liberty, and happiness of individuals and societies reflects his attempt to replace metaphysical considerations with physical ones, and otherworldly matters with political ones, which are changeable and ephemeral by their nature. Laws suitable for one people may not be suitable for another, and laws that help preserve one regime may be ruinous to another. Montesquieu, in short, encourages lawgivers to consider what is fitting and appropriate for individual constitutions and peoples, rather than to apply universal standards and precepts to individual political arrangements.[16] This theme carries over into Book IV of *The Spirit of Laws*, which is dedicated to political and civic education. Montesquieu advises that, since all laws are relative to the government in question, education ought to conform to the particular form of government and to the principle that animates it. To the extent that legislators ignore this advice and promote mores and practices that are in tension with the principle of government, then the given political order is subject to corruption and decline.[17]

Montesquieu aims at a comprehensive account of civic education, one that rivals Aristotle's and begs comparison with it. Montesquieu and Aristotle agree that the regime determines the nature of education, but they disagree on how to define regimes (which Montesquieu calls "governments") and on the overall purpose of doing so. Montesquieu identifies three kinds of government: republics, monarchies, and despotisms. In republics, some or most of the people rule; in monarchies, one alone rules but abides by the rule of law; and in despotisms, the whims and caprices of one alone rules all.[18] Unlike Aristotle, Montesquieu does not distinguish among regimes based on whether rulers govern for their own sake or for the sake of the ruled (or for some common good), nor does he pose the question of which regime is best and most appropriate for developing human virtue and excellence. For Montesquieu, virtue is merely the "principle" or the passion that animates republicanism. As each government has a nature or institutional architecture, so too does each government have a specific principle. In each case, the principle is a set of human passions that breathes life into the government in question. Virtue animates republics; honor fuels monarchy; and fear is the motor of despotism.

Virtue, which Aristotle argues is moral or intellectual human excellence, becomes for Montesquieu the passion that allows republicanism to survive. The dignity of self-rule does not impress Montesquieu, nor does he suggest that it is somehow a prerequisite for living a good and fulfilling human life.[19] Interestingly, in Montesquieu's presentation republics are the only regimes that rely on civic virtue, and are, in a way, the only governments that require very great attention to education.[20] By contrast, despotisms require no education, as the extreme obedience necessary from subjects or slaves in despotism is best cultivated through ignorance.[21] Yet, according to Montesquieu, the education in virtue on which republics depend is not representative of any kind of excellence. It is love of the laws and the homeland, or a passion for the public good at the expense of the private good. It represents a negation of the self (*renoncement à soi-même*) that Montesquieu declares to be uniformly painful, difficult, and unpleasant.[22] This self-sacrificing posture is not taught by way of moral education, but comes about as a result of denying or being denied our own naturally occurring individual passions. Montesquieu's famous analogy between monastic life and republicanism is worth quoting in full for all that it reveals:

> The less we can satisfy our particular passions, the more we give ourselves over to general ones. Why do monks love their order so much? It is through the same mechanism that makes their order unbearable (*insupportable*). Their rule deprives them of all the things that feed ordinary passions. There remains, then, this passion for the very rule that afflicts them. The more austere it is, that is to say, the more it suppresses their inclinations, the more it gives force to those allowed to them.[23]

Montesquieu's proto-Freudian account of the economy of the passions suggests that true self-sacrifice and heroism are not possible. Those who take great risks for seemingly little reward—like the great Spartan heroes who could have no individual honors—must be prevented from satisfying any of their particular passions or private interests.

Montesquieu emphasizes the very great difficulty of establishing and maintaining civic virtue in republics. Founders and legislators, crucial to the success of republican political life, must find or establish equality of property in a small territory; institute appropriate mechanisms for the maintenance of mores (e.g., censors); encourage respect for elders; and make it so that participation in politics is neither too egalitarian nor too hierarchical. Virtue itself is a feeling and not the result of knowledge, such that even the lowest citizen is capable of it. But, since the sentiment of virtue goes against the grain of our naturally individual interests, its inculcation depends on a radical manipulation of the passions.[24] While Montesquieu compliments ancient republicanism for its great feats (which he says would astonish the "small souls" of modern men), he leaves the reader wondering whether the effort to keep republicanism going—at least in its ancient form—is worth the trouble.[25] This is especially clear when he concludes that ancient republics were at odds with the development of commerce and other gentle arts, and that dedication to the public good resulted in human beings who at best were courageous and at worst were savage.[26]

Montesquieu begins to wean the reader away from the classical republican model by contrasting it with monarchy in the early books of *The Spirit of Laws*. Monarchic honor, although by no means without its problems, serves as a foil to republican virtue. Honor, the principle of monarchy, makes use of our self-love. Honor, the prejudice of each person and each rank together with the ambition natural to this sort of self-love, unintentionally contributes to the perpetuation of monarchy. Montesquieu makes much of the observation that monarchies accomplish a great deal through the personal ambitions of subjects, without having to make the excruciating efforts required to inculcate virtue in republics. In monarchy, each person works for the common good believing that he works for his personal good.[27] Monarchy ultimately falls short of protecting individual liberty and is too prone to degenerating into despotism, but it captures some of the modern science of politics that depends on the notion that we can harness individual interest for the public good.[28]

Ancient republicans were not privy to the modern science of politics, and modern monarchists failed to appreciate the nature of their government and what would be required to improve upon it. The only government to make political liberty its aim, and whose constitution came close to embodying the new mechanistic science of politics is that of England in Montesquieu's estimation. Political liberty, properly understood, is the security or opinion of security of individuals. The protection of individual liberty is possible only when government upholds the rule of law, and the power of government is checked and balanced by a separation of

powers. When legislative power and executive power are joined together—as they always are in ancient republics and modern monarchies—
liberty is precarious.[29] Part republic, part monarchy, and all commerce,
England and its separation of powers, its respect for the private lives of
subjects, the rule of law that allows for security in commercial and other
transactions, all point to the modern commercial republic.[30] In England,
the constitution helps foster mores that are in line with the preservation
of political liberty.[31]

Montesquieu does not explicitly outline how to uphold the laws and
mores of this free people, or how to emulate them in establishing and
maintaining them elsewhere. This does not mean that he was not acutely
aware of the many conditions for liberty and the great difficulty in de-
signing institutions and making them loved and obeyed. Although all the
springs of government are passions or a combination of passions, only
despotisms rely on untutored passions devoid of any institutional mas-
terminding. Modern liberty was born of the free mores and institutions of
the German conquerors of Rome, but a lack of understanding of the
underlying principles of this freedom had almost caused the denizens of
European absolute monarchies to lose this precious inheritance. Our natural liberty must be understood and instantiated by prudent statesmen:

> In order to form a moderate government, one must combine powers,
> regulate them, temper them, make them move; one must give one pow-
> er a ballast, so to speak, to make it possible for it to resist another; this is
> a masterpiece of legislation, that chance rarely brings about, and pru-
> dence is rarely permitted to produce.[32]

In lieu of an education that stresses either virtue or honor, Montesquieu
wants Frenchmen to relearn liberty and for the English to maintain theirs.

LEARNING AND MAINTAINING MODERN LIBERTY

How does one learn liberty? The barbaric freedom-loving mores of the
Germans are cultivated into the law-abiding and commercial love of freedom in modern England. The English, like other modern peoples, needed
not only to polish barbarous mores, but also to be set free from "destructive prejudices." Montesquieu comments that the English nation became
commercial once peace and liberty helped cure it of these destructive
prejudices.[33] The English threw off the oppressive baggage of history,
namely the twin influences of Aristotle and Christianity, that stood in the
way of embracing the acquisitive passions and the contractual sense of
justice that accompany commercial mores. When describing the manner
in which Jews freed themselves and their property from the vagaries of
political power by inventing the letter of exchange, Montesquieu gives
King John as the example of greedy monarch using and abusing Chris-

tian injunctions against commerce to steal property from disenfranchised Jews.[34] King John's rule is otherwise famous for provoking the ire of the nobility who came up with the Magna Charta to constrain the unlimited power of the monarchy. Limited rule and the ingenious invention of instruments of exchange that put property out of the reach of monarchs made possible the modern liberal commercial republic that England became.

Montesquieu gives an account of the ways in which the passionate pursuit of self-interest would provide an excellent foundation for political liberty.[35] He argues that assiduous attention to one's interests could temper many of the ill effects of previous versions of republicanism. For instance, he praises the invention of representative government, which tempers the people's participation in the business of governing.[36] The people are willing to give up direct democracy in part because they continue to have an indirect say in government, but also because they are busy looking out for their own welfare and enrichment. Partisanship replaces political participation. The concern each person has for his private welfare leads the people as a whole to mind their own business, but also to check the growth of power of the legislative and executive branches of government in turn.[37] This sort of activism does not require knowledge, only a healthy love of liberty. The rule of law and the equality that this implies elevates each individual to the level of petty monarch and gives him a certain pride.[38] While this means that Englishmen are fellow confederates rather than fellow citizens, equality under the laws and the ability to engage securely in improving one's lot gives everyone a stake in maintaining the institutions, laws, and practices that ensure the preservation of the modern commercial republic.

Montesquieu claims that undistorted (if well-directed) self-love is a sufficient basis for patriotism in commercial republics, effectively replacing the need for civic virtue in ancient republics. Loving the nation by inculcating virtue and enforcing uniform mores and customs is replaced by an ultimately harmonious cacophony of individual passions, which strengthens rather than weakens the modern commercial republic. Individuals join together in common cause when necessary:

> This nation would love its liberty prodigiously, because this liberty would be true; and it could happen that, to defend this liberty, it would sacrifice its goods, its comfort, its interests; and that it would impose very harsh taxes on itself, ones that even the most absolute monarch would not dare make his subjects bear.[39]

Maintaining real liberty is worth personal sacrifices. It turns out that the people, so ill-equipped to carry out the business of government according to Montesquieu, are capable judges of their own interests. They are willing to sacrifice their money and their ease when liberty is at stake, presumably because they understand that they might lose everything if they cannot keep conquerors at bay.

Commercial republicans do not aim at war, for their utilitarian sensibilities are not stirred by considerations of glory. They do, however, recognize the value of strong defense, and appreciate the risks that military men take in protecting the nation.[40] If this nation were to establish any kind of empire, Montesquieu muses, it would be for the sake of commerce rather than domination. England and like nations would not necessarily be peace-loving, particularly when it came to their numerous small, particular interests, and their jealousy in beholding the prosperity of others, but war would not be the exalted occupation that it had been for both ancient republics and monarchies.[41] The softness of mores that goes together with commerce changes the nature of men's ambitions, but does not make them too soft or too cloistered to attend to matters of political importance and to do what is necessary to maintain free institutions and mores.

England's continued enjoyment of liberty depends on maintaining its institutions and its free mores. The preservation of institutions, in turn, requires at least a little bit of old-fashioned reverence for the laws. Writing about the English constitutional monarchy, Montesquieu concludes that the legislative body should treat the monarch—the executive power—as "sacred."[42] If the legislature can judge the monarch's conduct, then there is a danger that executive power will shrink and become overwhelmed by legislative power. The power of the monarch, though correctly diluted in the Glorious Revolution, must still have the respect of the people. As many aspiring Montesquieuian reformers in eighteenth-century England concluded, education focusing on classical history ought to be replaced by a genuinely English education that looks to national politics, history, and mores. This was thought to help instill in Englishmen a love of English liberty and an appreciation for the great complexities and benefits of inherited institutions.[43]

Montesquieu understands, however, that the spirit of modern liberty does not easily accommodate itself to reverential respect for institutions, history, and authority. England, which bore the marks of both monarchy and republicanism, was least monarchic in its disdain for intermediary bodies like the nobility and its even more profound disdain for hereditary prerogatives.[44] Montesquieu argues that it would be good for the English to maintain the prerogatives of the nobility, and to allow for the continued existence of the House of Lords, but notes that these privileges are by their nature "odious"—perhaps this negative assessment of inherited privileges is meant to reflect English sensibilities rather than his own.[45] There is a tension, in other words, between the English "prodigious" love of freedom and the need to respect the institutions through which English liberty took shape.[46] Montesquieu hopes that diligently tending to their individual interests will keep the people from being overly involved in politics in a way that would erode obedience to laws and respect for lawmakers and executors of the law.

He recognizes, however, that the people may in fact become paranoid about encroachments on their liberty. In the case of the English, their characteristic impatience and worry makes them suited to liberty, but also makes them somewhat constitutionally unhappy and likely to perceive oppression where there is none.[47] Montesquieu is even more concerned about the opposite malady arising, which is to say the corruption of the spirit of liberty without which a country like England might become enslaved. He advises that the English constitution (or one like it) would perish when legislative power is more corrupt than executive power.[48] Sharon Krause argues convincingly that the corruption of the legislature would likely consist in its venality, which is to say its willingness to sell votes to the crown.[49] One must guard against the freewheeling English passions becoming fanatically political *and* too complacent about liberty.

The best way to avoid these problems is for legislators, statesmen, and citizens to be aware that although liberal regimes are ones in which our natural desires are most at home, good governments and liberal mores do not occur spontaneously. A liberal system of laws and mores is like complicated machinery that requires able tinkerers. Although Montesquieu chooses to emphasize the naturalness or the artlessness of the English regime, which sprouted forth in the forests of Germany, a considered analysis of his account of England uncovers the importance of purposive action in cultivating and maintaining what might have come about through chance.[50]

Legislators loom large in Montesquieu's recounting of ancient republicanism, but fade from view when discussing all other regimes, including England's. Montesquieu himself emerges as a true legislator in the sense that he teaches the nature and principles of the commercial republic so that they might be used to preserve and improve upon England and other future regimes that take political liberty as their aim. He repeatedly discourages would-be legislators from applying general principles without understanding particular circumstances, but he never concludes that changes, even major ones, are impossible. Great changes ought to be made only under the right conditions and with prudence.[51] Montesquieu, then, encourages a new kind of reverence for good legislators. He does not assimilate legislators to gods; he does not affirm the primacy of the old over the new; and, finally, he does not preach about the pure motives of great legislators. On the contrary, he emphasizes that legislators never have pure or objective motives, but are human beings whose "passions and prejudices" inform their lawgiving efforts.[52] Legislators, for better and for worse, are part of the legacy of each nation.[53] If not revered, legislators should be respected for their prudence in applying the principles of government to their particular situation. And to the extent that legislators fail or are perceived to fail in providing the best laws, enlightened citizens of commercial republics might at least appreciate the efforts of these legislators. Disappointment and righteous indignation at the perceived failures of our idols—our founders—might be tempered by the realization that building, rebuilding, and even tinkering with the machinery of government are onerous tasks.

Modern political liberty requires that citizens love their own particular laws, but it also calls for a seemingly opposed cosmopolitan education. As we recall, the tight civic bonds created by education in ancient republics made men into citizens in a manner that estranged them from humanity. Commerce offers a correction to the fanatical patriotism of virtuous republican citizenship, according to Montesquieu. "Commerce has spread the knowledge of the mores of all nations everywhere: mores have been compared to one another, and great things have resulted from this." Commerce corrupts the pure mores of the ancient republic, and "polishes and softens barbarous mores."[54] Trading nations typically have porous borders, even if they do engage in protectionism and other practices that give their own merchants and governments advantages over others. Commerce helps to erode the religious and other mores that stand in its way, and inculcates a humane outlook toward human beings *qua* human beings. Pride in particular institutions and mores is mixed with a gentle outlook toward the ways of life of others. This necessarily erodes the differences among peoples that would typically lead to war. England, Montesquieu writes, makes its political interests give way to its commercial ones.[55]

Together with the cosmopolitan education inherent in commercial mores, Montesquieu's own narrative approach in *The Spirit of Laws* points to another component of an education in liberalism: comparative politics and sociology. Montesquieu teaches us about the nature of politics by providing historical, cultural, geographical, and even geological accounts of various expressions of liberty (and its absence) across time and space. He does not forego universals, but comes to general conclusions by way of particular examples. The reader learns of the possibilities for and limits of liberty in different parts of the world. As we learn about the numerous obstacles to liberty, we also gain an education in countering illiberal forces where possible. Among other consequences, this approach encourages a broad analysis of political phenomena, which cannot but discourage myopia with respect to one's own nation. Cross-cultural and cross-historical analysis, which does not posit a model regime or ideal civilization (but, rather, the imperfect example of England), creates a liberal mindset in which cultural exchange, travel, and a gentle demeanor regarding the strange and unfamiliar are valued.

Montesquieu does not take the radical multicultural stance that there is inherent worth in all expressions of mores. He does, however, walk a fine line between nascent nationalism and cosmopolitan mores. For Montesquieu, the worth of institutions, mores, customs, manners, and so forth is derived from whether these fundamentally protect the individual and provide for security and liberty. Superstitions that lead to oppression or convince human beings to forego their interests are not compatible with liberal mores and ought not to be allowed. Montesquieu would not be sympathetic to attempts to permit any and all practices in the name of individual choice. Polygamy, for example, would count as illiberal for the oppression of women in this household arrangement and the despotic effects on husbands of multiple wives.[56] Similarly, Montesquieu—a proponent of religious toleration—suggests that any religion that seeks to impose itself on others (even non-violently), which includes any new religions, ought to be banned.[57] Montesquieu's comparative education and the thrust of his cosmopolitanism are meant to be in the service of forming our judgment with respect to the compatibility and incompatibility of various practices with liberty.

TENSIONS BETWEEN LIBERALISM AND CIVIC EDUCATION

Montesquieu has much to teach us about how to build and sustain liberal institutions and mores. We ought to encourage the love of these institutions and mores, which are, in a sense, easy to love because they conduce to our own good. As Montesquieu says with respect to the English, they love and protect their liberty because theirs is true liberty. As I have argued, Montesquieu also chastens us to appreciate the need for human prudence and wise legislation in the service of protecting our political liberty. Civic education, then, entails teaching the principles of free government. But, as the reality of low civic engagement in contemporary America suggests, our natural interest in protecting our liberty is not compelling enough to result in an engaged and vigilant citizenry.

In an important sense Montesquieu was well aware of this problem, even though he did not give voice to it the way Tocqueville did a couple of generations later. Montesquieu's Englishmen are not written in such a way as to be simply endearing to the reader. They are petty, unsociable, equal parts bashful and proud, miserable, mercenary, restless, fickle, debauched with respect to their relations with women (while their wives live a cloistered life), and undisciplined in their passions.[58] Part of the point of this unflattering portrayal is to emphasize that monarchic refinement and even ancient heroism are but skin deep; English character may not be beautiful, but their liberty is real and solid. Still, their liberty rings somewhat hollow if it means that liberal politics makes human beings less grand, less elegant, and deaf to the call of virtue. Lacking an appreciation for higher things, it is not difficult to see how commercial mores can devolve into love of money at the expense of love of liberty, nor is it hard to imagine that the public realm—which explicitly exists for the sake of the private one—might dissolve entirely. Furthermore, the tight rope between proto-nationalism or love of one's own institutions and cosmopolitanism may be a difficult one to walk. Fanatical nationalism and tepid supranational sentiments are possible outcomes, both of which endanger liberal regimes.

Although Montesquieu recognizes some of the limitations of liberal government, perhaps he underestimates the need to counteract these limitations and to ennoble liberalism. As the commercial republic requires some self-government, so it requires a modicum of virtue.[59] In other words, Montesquieu may exaggerate the differences between ancient and modern liberty, and the extent to which the new science of the interests might replace the need for civic virtue. The Anti-Federalists echo this concern in the American context, as they considered whether the emphasis on individual profit in large commercial republics would not undermine the constitutional order that helps guarantee liberty.[60] Indeed, many during the Founding era paid careful attention to the importance of civic education in liberal society. Most famously, Thomas Jefferson worked toward local participation in education and established state institutions that would provide a secular education with special emphasis on Lockean and Montesquieuian principles of government.[61] In short, America has always represented a mix between liberalism and republicanism. It is quite likely that this unorthodox mix (in Montesquieu's view) is responsible for its success.

Montesquieu, then, is a strange oracle for us to consult. On the one hand, he mostly dismisses the need for political virtue in modern commercial republics. On the other hand, a close analysis of his account of the prerequisites for liberty makes clear that much effort, prudence, and education are needed to foster liberal mores and institutions. Yet this effort is in the service of forming human beings that are, in some way, less impressive than ones of bygone eras. Montesquieu does, however, suggest that a certain kind of greatness is possible in liberal societies, a true greatness that was elusive under earlier forms of government. What liberal societies lack in taste, they more than make up for in their originality and inventiveness. With the power of a Michelangelo rather than the grace of a Raphael, Englishmen and other rude, semi-barbarous free people might exhibit a new kind of strength, born of their independence of body and mind.[62] This might be Montesquieu's most important praise of liberal mores, and may serve as a positive point of departure to reaffirm liberal politics. Liberty-loving citizens are willing to turn their satirical and somewhat antisocial eye on themselves to engage in healthy introspection about the imperfections of their regime.[63] This sort of independence and strength of mind, translated into self-conscious examination and reexamination of one's cherished ways and institutions, is the engine that makes possible the preservation of liberty.

NOTES

1. See, for example, Robert D. Putnam, *Bowling Alone* (New York: Simon & Schuster, 2000) and David E. Campbell, *Why We Vote: How Schools and Communities Shape Our Civic Life* (Princeton: Princeton University Press, 2006). Putnam focuses on membership in voluntary associations and Campbell on public choice, but both note and study the issue of American disengagement from public life. Putnam's book is a bestseller, and this title "Bowling Alone" became an anthem for the absence of political community.

2. Alexis de Tocqueville, *Democracy in America*, trans. and ed. Harvey C. Mansfield, and Delba Winthrop (Chicago: University of Chicago Press, 2000), II.1.1.

3. Amy Gutmann gives a powerful account of the type of virtues necessary to live in a pluralistic and democratic society. Amy Gutmann, "Why Should Schools Care about Civic Education?" in *Rediscovering the Democratic Purposes of Education*, ed. Lorraine M. McDonnell, P. Michael Timpane, and Roger Benjamin (Lawrence: University Press of Kansas, 2000), 73–90.

4. Charles Francis Adams, ed., *The Works of John Adams*, 10 vols. (Boston: Little, Brown, 1850–56), 4:292.

5. Thomas L. Pangle, *The Ennobling of Democracy* (Baltimore: Johns Hopkins University Press, 1992), 150–51.

6. Walter Berns, "The Cultivation of Citizenship," in *Public Morality, Civic Virtue, and the Problem of Modern Liberalism*, ed. T. William Boxx and Gary M. Quinlivan (Grand Rapids, MI: William B. Eerdmans Publishing Co., 2000), 2; Paul Carrese, "Montesquieu's Complex Natural Right and Moderate Liberalism: The Roots of American Moderation," *Polity* 36 (January 2004): 247, 249.

7. It is important not to overstate the difference between the Federalists and the Anti-Federalists. The former did not dismiss the importance of public-spiritedness and the latter did not propose that ancient republican virtue be revived wholesale. See Herbert J. Storing, *What the Anti-Federalists Were For* (Chicago: University of Chicago Press, 1981), 71–76.

8. Alexander Hamilton, *The Federalist* No. 9.

9. *Spirit of Laws*, XIX.27, ¶62. All references from *The Spirit of Laws* are from *Oeuvres Complètes*, ed. Roger Caillois (Paris: Gallimard, 1951), and will be given by book, chapter, and, when the chapter is lengthy, paragraph number. Translations are mine.

10. *Persian Letters*, letters 133–37. All references of the *Persian Letters* are from *Oeuvres complètes*, ed. Roger Caillois (Paris: Editions Gallimard, Bibliothèque de la Pléiade, 1949). Translations are my own, and citations reflect letter numbers, as Montesquieu assigned them.

11. *Persian Letters*, letter 136.

12. Cf. *Spirit of Laws*, XI.6 ¶67.

13. *Persian Letters*, letter 136.

14. *Persian Letters*, letter 133.

15. *Spirit of Laws*, I.3.

16. For how this might undermine divine law, see especially *The Spirit of Laws*, XXVI.9.

17. *Spirit of Laws*, III.11.

18. *Spirit of Laws*, II.1.

19. *Spirit of Laws*, XI.2.

20. *Spirit of Laws*, IV.5.

21. *Spirit of Laws*, IV.3.

22. *Spirit of Laws*, IV.5. The word Montesquieu uses is *pénible*.

23. *Spirit of Laws*, V.2.

24. *Spirit of Laws*, V.2.

25. *Spirit of Laws*, IV.4.

26. *Spirit of Laws*, IV.8; book IX *in toto*; XI.5; XXI.7. See also David Lowenthal, "Montesquieu and the Classics: Republican Government in *The Spirit of the Laws*," in *Ancients and Moderns*, ed. Joseph Cropsey (New York: Basic Books, 1964), 258–87.

27. *Spirit of Laws*, III.7; see also III.5–6.

28. See Andrea Radasanu, "Montesquieu on Moderation, Monarchy and Reform," *History of Political Thought* 31 (Summer 2010): 283–307.

29. *Spirit of Laws*, XI.6 ¶4.

30. There is some disagreement among Montesquieu scholars with respect to whether his England is a monarchy or a republic. There is also disagreement about whether England represents Montesquieu's preferred form of government. On the first point, as I already state, Montesquieu suggests that England is neither monarchy nor (ancient) republic. In my reading, it is a departure from both, a new form of government that he does not label. "Commercial republic" comes closest to Montesquieu's presentation by emphasizing the importance of commerce and taking into account equality under the law present in this regime. On the second point, as I bring out later in this chapter, England is certainly unappealing on a number of levels. Still, I argue that Montesquieu is positively inclined to its constitutional arrangement and love of liberty. For interpreters who understand Montesquieu as monarchist, see, for example, Sharon Krause, *Liberalism with Honor* (Cambridge, MA: Harvard University Press, 2002); Michael Mosher, "Monarchy's Paradox: Honor in the Face of Sovereign Power," in *Montesquieu's Science of Politics: Essays on the Spirit of the Laws*, ed. David W. Carrithers, Michael A. Mosher, and Paul Rahe (Lanham, MD: Rowman and Littlefield, 2001); Céline Spector, *Montesquieu: Pouvoirs, richesses et sociétés* (Paris: Éditions Hermann, 2004). For Montesquieu's England as modern commercial republic see, Thomas Pangle, *Montesquieu's Philosophy of Liberalism* (Chicago: University of Chicago Press, 1973); Paul Rahe, *Montesquieu and the Logic of Liberty* (New Haven: Yale University Press, 2010).

31. *Spirit of Laws*, XIX.26.

32. *Spirit of Laws*, V.14.

33. *Spirit of Laws*, XIX.27, ¶29.

34. *Spirit of Laws*, XXI.20.

35. Spector argues that Montesquieu finds the science of interests lacking and so opts for something like liberal honor. Céline Spector, "Honor, Interest, Virtue: The Affective Foundations of the Political in *The Spirit of Laws*," in *Montesquieu and His Legacy*, ed. Rebecca E. Kingston (Albany: SUNY Press, 2008), 69. On the other end of interpretation, some argue that commercial mores represent more than just self-interest well understood. See, for example, Robert Howse, "Montesquieu on Commerce, Conquest, War, and Peace," *Brooklyn Journal of International Law* 693 (2006): 15–16. On this reading, commercial mores are the gateway to a new cosmopolitan morality, and the ethic of reciprocity that these mores engender soars beyond its tawdry mercenary beginnings. I argue that he is neither as negative about self-interest as Spector and others suggest, nor as hopeful about its ability to transcend itself and become the basis of an other-regarding morality as Howse and others would maintain.

36. *Spirit of Laws*, XI.6, ¶24; see also XIX.27 ¶63.

37. *Spirit of Laws*, XIX.27, ¶4.

38. *Spirit of Laws*, XIX.27, ¶62; see also ¶53.

39. *Spirit of Laws*, XIX.27, ¶23.

40. *Spirit of Laws*, XIX.27, ¶28.

41. *Spirit of Laws*, XIX.27, ¶32 ff.

42. *Spirit of Laws*, XI.6, ¶45.

43. F. T. H. Fletcher, "Montesquieu and British Education in the Eighteenth Century," *Modern Language Review* 38 (October 1943): 306.

44. *Spirit of Laws*, II.4.

45. *Spirit of Laws*, XI.6, ¶33.

46.   Perhaps Montesquieu believes that modern liberty, like ancient liberty, can become the love of extreme equality and the eschewal of all law and authority. Cf. *Spirit of Laws*, VIII.3.

47.   *Spirit of Laws*, XIV.13.

48.   *Spirit of Laws*, XI.6, ¶68.

49.   Krause points out that Montesquieu refers to this practice in his unpublished *Notes sur l'Angleterre*. Montesquieu reflects that this venality is unworthy of liberty. Sharon Krause, "The Uncertain Inevitability of Decline in Montesquieu," *Political Theory* 30 (October 2002): 717–18.

50.   *Spirit of Laws*, XI.6, ¶67.

51.   *Spirit of Laws*, XXIX.13.

52.   *Spirit of Laws*, XXIX.19.

53.   *Spirit of Laws*, I.3.

54.   *Spirit of Laws*, XX.1.

55.   *Spirit of Laws*, XX.7.

56.   *Spirit of Laws*, XVI.9. See also the seraglio tale in the *Persian Letters*.

57.   *Spirit of Laws*, XXV.9, 10.

58.   *Spirit of Laws*, XIX.27, ¶61, 66.

59.   A new trend in Montesquieu scholarship is to suggest that the dichotomy between liberalism and republicanism is imposed on him. E.g., Céline Spector, "Montesquieu: Critique of Republicanism?" in *Republicanism: History, Theory and Practice*, ed. Daniel Weinstock and Christian Nadeau (London: Frank Cass Publishers, 2004), 38–53. Spector argues that Pocock and Skinner both use Montesquieu to their own ends, neither appreciating sufficiently that liberal and republican categories are a foreign imposition on him and his work (39). In my reading, Montesquieu goes to some lengths to separate liberal government from republican government. That said, I agree with Spector that there are republican components to Montesquieu's modern liberalism, and I argue here that—perhaps more than he realized—his liberalism depends on republican virtues.

60.   Storing, *What the Anti-Federalists Were For*, 73.

61.   For thorough and excellent accounts of this, see Berns, "The Cultivation of Citizenship," 3–5 and Pangle, *The Ennobling of Democracy*, 132–73.

62.   *Spirit of Laws*, XIX.27 ¶73.

63.   *Spirit of Laws*, XIX.27 ¶70–71.

II

The Changing Landscape of American Civic Life

FOUR

American Amnesia

Bruce Cole

A proper recognition of how America's past continues to shape our present is vital for responsible citizenship and the health of our nation. The national tragedy of September 11th caused many Americans to question who we were as a nation and what our values were. For a brief moment, we sought to unify ourselves through a rediscovery and reassertion of America's founding principles and ideals. When I became Chairman of the National Endowment for the Humanities (NEH) in December 2001, the agency responded to the crisis by instituting a national program to improve the teaching and understanding of American history. Called "We the People,"[1] the effort was launched by President George W. Bush in a Rose Garden ceremony, and ultimately garnered about 90 million new dollars in congressional appropriations. The widespread support for "We the People" was predicated on the belief that reconnecting with our past could enable us to reassert our national identity.

History is an essential part of our mental apparatus; it is our fourth dimension. As William Faulkner famously said, "The past is never dead. It's not even past."[2] Memory is an essential part of human life because, regardless of our awareness or recognition of its influence, it informs our daily decisions. Like individuals, our nation also has a collective memory that informs our lives as citizens.

Knowledge of our history is central to the character of our citizens and our nation and so it is worrisome that the teaching of U.S. history is in grave decline. Take, for example, North Carolina, where education officials seem to believe that the past is beyond dead; it is not even the past. In 2010, bureaucrats from the state's Department of Public Instruction recommended that high school students stop studying U.S. history before

1877.[3] Defenders of this dubious proposal claimed that recent history was more relevant and interesting to students. Rebecca Garland, the chief academic officer for North Carolina's Department of Public Instruction, insisted that they were "not trying to go away from American history" but rather to "figure out a way to teach it where students are connected to it, where they see the big idea, where they are able to make connections and draw relationships between parts of our history and the present day."[4]

The desire to appeal to students' interests, which looked innocuous, provoked a storm of outrage from North Carolinians who sent over seven thousand emails and letters to officials protesting the curriculum changes. The spectrum of incensed and offended respondents ranged from one professor who described the idea to start history at 1877 as a major step backward, to a local school board member who claimed to be "ashamed about any curriculum that leaves out the Founding Fathers and the creation of our Constitution," to a Tea Party member who described the proposal as "yet another incremental step in the progressive movement to abandon the principles on which our nation was built." Even Governor Beverly Perdue said that she was surprised anybody would want to take out this core history content.[5]

Governor Perdue was right; excluding events prior to 1877—the Mayflower Compact, the original Tea Party, the American Revolution, the Declaration of Independence and the Constitution, the Civil War, and Reconstruction—from high school curricula would be tantamount to ignoring early American history. North Carolina's new social studies standards would replace instruction in those centuries before 1877 with an exploration of contemporary international relations, human rights struggles, America's global conflicts, and an understanding of how changes in physical environment have impacted American society, among other things. Educators would emphasize late nineteenth- and twentieth-century political and social movements, while students would be asked to critique their outcome. In other words, trendy history-lite.

The dust up over North Carolina's recommended curricular change made national news. In response to the firestorm of outrage, school officials said that they would increase the number of pre-high school classes; however, they offered no details as to how they would do so. In defense of the changes, June Atkinson, the state superintendent of the Public Schools of North Carolina, insisted that even under the new proposal, "Events, people, and dates that are so familiar to many of us will still be taught to students."[6] Really? Citizens, parents, educators, and administrators alike must have been wondering which events, people, and dates we know so well. According to the facts, not very many.

American adults are far less "familiar" with American history than Superintendent Atkinson would have us believe. According to a 2009 survey published by the American Revolution Center (ARC), 83 percent of adult Americans failed an exam covering basic facts about the American Revolution and the Founding, scoring an average of 44 percent.[7] Colleges and universities are not doing much to alleviate Americans' amnesia. According to a 2007 survey conducted by the Intercollegiate Studies Institute (ISI) of 14,000 freshman and seniors in fifty major research universities and four-year colleges nationwide, the average freshman scored only 51 percent on a basic test of American history, politics, and economics, while the average senior only marginally improved to 54 percent on the same test.[8] Perhaps even more troubling is that many of these graduating seniors exhibited what the study terms "negative learning," that is, they knew *less* about American history after four years of college than they did upon entering these institutions of higher learning.

The situation of America's increasing ignorance of its own history is just as alarming among K–12 students, according to the most recent Nation's Report Card, the National Assessment of Educational Progress (NAEP), administered by the U.S. Department of Education to fourth, eighth, and twelfth graders. In 2006, 30 percent of fourth graders, 35 percent of eighth graders, and 53 percent of twelfth graders performed only at the basic level in American history, which is the lowest possible score.[9] It seems that the longer students stay in school, the less they know about history.

So how did all this happen? The North Carolina history debate can shed some light on this epidemic of historical ignorance. The state's current standards are just as worrisome as the new proposal to eliminate history prior to 1877. Only one of the state's twelve competency goals focuses on the period before 1789. Thus, North Carolina's curriculum generally does not cover the French and Indian War, the Stamp Act, the Boston Tea Party, the Declaration of Independence, the U.S. Constitution, *The Federalist Papers*, and the Revolutionary War itself. Instead, it begins with the period from 1789 to 1820, encouraging students to "identify, investigate, and assess the effectiveness of the institutions of the emerging republic." The three objectives for that period of American history are:

1. Identify the major domestic issues and conflicts experienced by the nation during the Federalist Period.
2. Analyze the political freedoms available to the following groups prior to 1820: women, wage earners, landless farmers, American Indians, African Americans, and other ethnic groups.
3. Assess commercial and diplomatic relationships with Britain, France, and other nations.[10]

Note that only one of these three fuzzy objectives actually focuses fully on American history. There is a good deal of material to cover, but too little of it focuses on *the major events* of American history. The standards neither encourage the rigorous engagement of primary sources, such as reading the actual texts of the founding documents, nor do they teach students the major ideas and philosophical rationales behind the Founding Fathers' decision to rebel against the most powerful empire on Earth. One would expect that students instructed under these curricular guidelines would have a difficult time understanding or explaining why the founders of this nation were willing to sacrifice *their lives, their fortunes and their sacred honor.*

North Carolina's new history proposal makes matters worse by relegating the study of the American Revolution only to a very elementary and rudimentary treatment in the pre-high school years. State education officials claim that this is an effort to "give students more study of United States history"[11] by adding two additional history courses—one in fifth grade and one in middle school—but the proposal still eliminates every historical event prior to 1877 in the eleventh grade. A fifth grader can hardly be expected to understand the subtleties of the French and Indian War or *The Federalist Papers* with the same depth as an eleventh grader, especially since we know from the Department of Education test (NAEP) that eleventh graders themselves are failing history. This proposal to teach these events only at the elementary school level—even if it means the addition of history courses—does not seem to make much sense if the goal is to improve America's historical deficit. Education officials in North Carolina devised a second draft of the social studies standards that includes a two-part, high school level United States history course; they are working on the problem and are trying to resolve it.

If one considers national public education standards, North Carolina's willingness to erase early American history from the collective memory of students is not an exception in the United States. Almost a decade ago, the Thomas B. Fordham Institute, a leading research foundation on K–12 education, found that three-fifths of the states had weak or ineffective U.S. history standards. This study examined historical content, sequential development (the building of knowledge from one grade to the next) in K–12, and the balance of history standards. Only six states received high standard grades; five received very good grades; and twenty-two states and the District of Columbia failed.[12] I would suggest that such results are not surprising given the absence of clear content-rich standards throughout the country. Moreover, despite many Americans' belief of the importance of learning American history, without high standards to which to refer, parents and taxpayers have no reliable way to hold teachers accountable for what students do or do not learn.

The findings of the Fordham Institute's 2011 follow-up study concludes that the standards of the nation's top universities have only exacerbated matters because fewer college students are required to study American history.[13] Only 10 percent of students at fifty-five elite colleges and universities, as ranked by *U.S. News and World Report*, are even required to take American history. The leading author of the Fordham Institute studies, Sheldon M. Stern, observes, "If students are not going to get the history in K–12, they're not going to get it at all."[14]

Nor are state-imposed high school history standards and the failure of our elite institutions to teach American history the only fundamental obstacles to overcoming our historical deficit. Professional standards for the teaching of history are also falling far short. In 1998, the National Board for Professional Teaching Standards (NBPTS) developed twelve standards of excellent teaching for the field of history. These included knowledge of students' cognitive, physical, and social development; valuing diversity; creating a dynamic learning environment; and "reflection," meaning reflecting on their practices and student performances. In 2010, NBPTS revised its standards, shrinking the number to eight.[15]

Of the original twelve standards, only two were related to actual history: having knowledge of the subject matter and developing a "civic competence." Under the 2010 revision of these standards, the latter has been combined with other standards into a single standard: "Developing Social Understanding, Engagement, and Civic Identity."[16]

The committee that revised the standards noted that "one of the most readily apparent changes" between the 1998 and the 2010 standards "is in the nature of detail found in the content standard." The committee "retains the commitment to subject matter knowledge as an indispensable characteristic of accomplished social studies-history teachers"; however, they "avoided [the] temptation" to try "to identify all the content that teachers in these fields need to master" because doing so would take up too much space in the standards and because most teachers work within the content guidelines of their states and school districts.[17] Thus, teachers are left to rely upon state content standards that may—if North Carolina school administrators had their way—eliminate half of the content!

If the state and professional standards fail to offer clear guidance to teachers who are supposed to foster students' knowledge and understanding of U.S. history, the nation's college and university standards for teacher preparation are abysmal. College students training to be K–12 history teachers are required to study minimal history, if at all; they need only complete a content-free education major. Furthermore, their curricular training seems to be one of the least rigorous tracks; they graduate with the fewest number of credit hours, minors, and double majors of almost any other discipline. Fortunately some states, such as Virginia, require college students to major in a content-centered discipline, such as history or government, in order to teach it—but not all states have such high standards or expectations for public school teachers. The unfortunate but not unexpected result is that high school history teachers have often been trained to coach athletics rather than teach history, and, without intending to denigrate coaches, one cannot teach what one does not know.

In addition to inadequate history standards and poor teacher preparation, textbooks are often light on subject matter, watered down on content, peppered with partisan perspectives, and written in a boring tone.
Education historian Diane Ravitch's book *The Language Police: How Pressure Groups Restrict What Students Learn* demonstrates that textbook committee reviewers prioritize "representational fairness," meaning the
avoidance of overrepresentation, underrepresentation, stereotyping, or
controversy relating to an ethnic, racial, gender, or national category.[18]
These reviewers are often uninformed by actual research findings or the
peer-review system, and often lack expertise on the historical content
they are evaluating. The quality of textbooks has thus become banal and
boring, rather than interesting and engaging, because they are put together piecemeal by partisan committees comprised of individuals who lack
the fortitude or skills to provide a coherent or consistent narrative history.

Fear of controversy—which is really a substantial part of the nature of
history—necessarily limits the content and inhibits the history textbook's
ability to inspire and energize the curiosity and interests of students.

History is exciting when taught well. Humans are already wired to be
interested in history, but it must be told well through exciting, energiz-
ing, and engaging textbooks, and taught by properly trained, intellectually knowledgeable, and actively engaged teachers. This is not what is
happening. The social and often political agendas of reviewers take pref-
erence over students' academic needs and enthusiasms. Moreover, these
reviewers are often paralyzed by fear of offending any particular community or group. The quality of textbooks suffers, and students often miss
out on an opportunity to become engaged with their national heritage.

The recent furor over the proposed adoption of controversial history
textbooks in Texas and Virginia could have widespread implications
across the country. Texas is one of the largest buyers of textbooks in the
country and it often disproportionately influences the textbook selection
of other states. Not unlike the fiery response against North Carolina's
recent curriculum proposal, the reaction in Texas indicates that many in
the American public refuse to allow our history standards to degenerate
further.[19] This is a positive sign.

By tracing the inadequate national standards for learning, teaching,
and textbooks, we discover a disturbing picture of the many forces that
are working against teaching American history well. Empirical data confirms that our nation is not doing an adequate job of teaching its own
history.

Let me conclude by suggesting some methods to get us out of this
mess that is our K–12 history education:

First, as the Fordham Institute study illustrates, educational standards for public schools must be reformed and teachers, schools, and students need to be held accountable by parents for the proper teaching and learning of their subjects. The standards themselves should be comprehensive and cover the most important political, social, cultural, and economic events and historical figures. They should be balanced; they should not be posturing or hagiographic. They should be historically correct, not politically correct. State standards should represent the entire story of American history—the center and the margins, the peaks and the valleys—all of it. Standards should foster a sense of narrative history, analytical thinking (which is a skill needed for the study of history), and excitement about why certain things happened.

For instance, students should be able to think critically about the role the Constitution plays in their lives.[20] Good teaching of the Constitution would get them thinking about some of the following questions: "Do you worship or not worship at an institution of your choice?" "Do you read newspaper editorials?" "Do you attend public gatherings?" "Do you vote?" "Do you see the peaceful transfer of power at the end of each election cycle?" Such inquiries could enable students to explore the direct impact of the U.S. Constitution on the way that they live. To understand the Constitution is to understand more than the words of the document themselves; it is to interrogate why Americans have certain rights and responsibilities, and why we need to exercise them. An adept teacher can begin to excite students—or adults—about eighteenth-century men in white wigs simply by discussing the direct impact of the Founding generation on the daily activities of the average American today.

The Fordham Institute study has also shown that California, Indiana, and Massachusetts were able to produce high-quality history standards because they were not overly dependent on faulty national standards; they included real subject matter; they involved leading experts and researchers in the process of writing the standards; they did not overload themselves with committee and stakeholder consensus; and they had leaders who fought for top standards. In developing the history and social studies standards, they emphasized *E Pluribus Unum* rather than multiculturalism, and resisted the pressure to include every student's heritage over a proper representation of the accomplishments, challenges, and missteps of history.

Second, teacher quality and training must be a priority. States must encourage a more rigorous subject-matter teacher preparation education at the college level. Without a degree in history and minors in other related fields like government or economics, high school social studies teachers will lack the primary source knowledge needed to provide a sophisticated treatment of history, rather than a partisan oversimplification. Accurate historical content must be the foundation for all teachers-in-training so that they can get the education they need and deserve to teach effectively.

Third, parents, the single-most influential factor in students' education, need to be involved. Research has shown that parent participation in their children's K–12 education is twice as predictive of students' academic success as socioeconomic status.[21] Not only can their participation produce students who are better motivated and more successful in the classroom, parent involvement will enable them to become better watchdogs of the content of their children's textbooks. When President Ronald Reagan left the Oval Office in 1989, he gave the traditional farewell address, which always has an admonition. The last part of his farewell address was about teaching American history. He correctly pointed to the central importance of parenting for fostering the proper civic awareness in our young adults when he said, "All great change in America begins at the dinner table. . . . [I]f your parents haven't been teaching you what it means to be an American, let 'em know and nail 'em on it. That would be a very American thing to do."[22] As decades of inadequate history standards are leading parents' memory of history to dwindle, and as each succeeding generation's standards are weakening, we risk losing sight of what it means to be American.

In conclusion, why should one care about American history? An answer requires us to turn to the Founders themselves. The Founders, who were in the process of making history, were passionate about the need to study history. They argued that one of the surest means of securing "the blessing of liberty to ourselves and our posterity" is by educating rising generations about their own history. George Washington echoed this sentiment in his first inaugural address: "[T]he preservation of the sacred fire of liberty, and the destiny of the republican model of government, are justly considered as *deeply*, perhaps as *finally* staked, on the experiment entrusted to the hands of the American people."[23] Benjamin Franklin's oft-repeated quote also comes to mind. When Franklin left Independence Hall after signing the Constitution—nobody yet knew what kind of government had been created—a woman asked him, "Well, Dr. Franklin, what have you given us—a monarchy or a republic?" Franklin famously replied, "A Republic—if you can keep it."

Beyond the belief and assertions of the Founders themselves that we need to preserve and study America's history, one still needs a substantive reason why such a study is important so as to not blindly idolize the nation's founding. The reason we need history is this: "We the people" are not united by blood, by land, or by race, but by the ideas, principles, and traditions upon which our republic was formed. We created our country on a shared creed—on the Declaration of Independence—which found its blueprint in the written Constitution. These documents and the ideas that bind them and the nation together can only be sustained by our enduring knowledge of and allegiance to them.

This is especially important as waves of immigrants come to our shores, something that has been a part of the American experience since the beginning. Twenty-first-century immigrants, like many of their predecessors, become Americans by their knowledge of and allegiance to the ideas and ideals which have held this nation together for centuries. But a democratic republic like ours is not self-sustaining. In order to thrive it requires understanding, commitment, and support of its citizens. As Thomas Jefferson warned, "If a nation expects to be ignorant and free, in a state of civilization, it expects what never was and never will be."[24] Our nation's future depends on its ability to transmit the knowledge of its institutions, its values, and the rights and responsibilities of its citizens. A people cannot defend what they cannot define.

In 1983, an aptly named report called *A Nation at Risk* took the country by storm. It concluded, "If an unfriendly foreign power had attempted to impose on America the mediocre educational performance that exists today, we might well have viewed it as an act of war. As it stands, we have allowed this to happen to ourselves."[25] Thirty years later, little has changed, and our American amnesia is as dangerous now as it was then.

NOTES

1. These programs included funding for films like Ken Burns's PBS documentary *The War*; cultural workshops in communities around the nation; the We the People Challenge Grant program, which promoted the teaching of American history at all levels of education; and "Picturing America," which provided high-quality reproductions of classic American art to schools and libraries throughout the country.

2. William Faulkner, *Requiem for a Nun*, act I, scene III.

3. "North Carolina Schools May Cut Chunk Out of U.S. History Lessons," February 3, 2010, available at www.foxnews.com/story/0,2933,584758,00.html (accessed November 14, 2011).

4. "North Carolina Schools May Cut."

5. Bruce Mildwurf, "How U.S. History Is Taught Could Change in N.C.," February 10, 2010, available online at www.wral.com/news/local/story/6997068/ (accessed May 30, 2012).

6. Public Schools of North Carolina State Board of Education/Department of Public Instruction, "NC's Draft Social Studies Curriculum Expands the Time Students Will Study U.S. History," February 3, 2010, available online at www.ncpublicschools.org/newsroom/news/2009-10/20100205-01 (accessed June 2, 2012).

7. American Revolution Center, *The American Revolution: Who Cares? Americans Are Yearning to Learn, Failing to Know* (Philadelphia: The American Revolution Center, 2009), available online at americanrevolutioncenter.org/sites/default/files/attachment/ARCv27_web.pdf (accessed June 5, 2012).

8. National Civic Literacy Board, *Failing Our Students, Failing America: Holding Colleges Accountable for Teaching America's History and Institutions* (Wilmington, DE: Intercollegiate Studies Institute, 2007), available online at www.americancivicliteracy.org/2007/summary_summary.html (accessed May 21, 2012).

9. Jihyun Lee and Andrew R. Weiss, *The Nation's Report Card: U.S. History, 2006* (NCES 2007–474) (Washington, DC: U.S. Government Printing Office for the U.S. Department of Education, National Center for Education Statistics, 2006), available online

at nationsreportcard.gov and nces.ed.gov/nationsreportcard/pdf/main2006/2007474. pdf (accessed January 12, 2012).

10. See North Carolina Standard Course of Study, available online at schoolcenter. gcsnc.com/education/components/scrapbook/default.php?sectiondetailid=309116& (accessed June 2, 2012).

11. North Carolina Department of Public Instruction, "NC's Draft Social Studies Curriculum Expands the Time Students Will Study U.S. History," available online at www.ncpublicschools.org/newsroom/news/2009-10/20100205-01 (accessed November 14, 2011).

12. Sheldon M. Stern, *Effective State Standards for U.S. History: A 2003 Report Card* (Washington, DC: Thomas B. Fordham Institute, 2003), available online at www. edexcellencemedia.net/publications/2003/200309_effectivestatestandardsforushistory/ History_Standards2003.pdf (accessed May 31, 2012).

13. See Sheldon M. Stern and Jeremy A. Stern, *The State of State U.S. History Standards, 2011* (Washington, DC: Thomas B. Fordham Institute, 2011), available online at www.edexcellencemedia.net/publications/2011/20110216_SOSHS/SOSS_History_ FINAL.pdf (accessed May 31, 2012).

14. Michelle D. Anderson, "Report Gives a Majority of States Poor Grades on History Standards," *Education Weekly*, available online at www.edweek.org/ew/articles/ 2011/02/16/21history.h30.html (accessed November 11, 2011).

15. National Board for Professional Teaching Standards, *Social Studies-History Standards for Teachers* (Arlington, VA: National Board for Professional Teaching Standards, 2001). The latest edition, *Social Studies-History Standards*, 2nd ed. (Arlington, VA: National Board for Professional Teaching Standards, 2010), is available online at www. nbpts.org/userfiles/file/SocialStudiesHistory_standards.pdf (accessed November 14, 2011).

16. NBPTS, *Social Studies-History Standards.*

17. NBPTS, *Social Studies-History Standards.*

18. Diane Ravitch, *The Language Police: How Pressure Groups Restrict What Students Learn* (New York: Knopf, 2003).

19. See Michael Birnbaum, "Historians Speak Out Against Proposed Texas Textbook Changes," *Washington Post*, March 18, 2010, available online at www. washingtonpost.com/wp-dyn/content/article/2010/03/17/AR2010031700560.html (accessed June 15, 2012); James McKinley Jr., "Texas Conservatives Win Curriculum Change," *New York Times*, March 12, 2010, available online at www.nytimes.com/2010/ 03/13/education/13texas.html (accessed June 15, 2012); and Kevin Sieff, "Virginia 4th-grade Textbook Criticized Over Claims on Black Confederate Soldiers," *Washington Post*, October 20, 2010, available online at www.washingtonpost.com/wp-dyn/content/ article/2010/10/19/AR2010101907974.html (accessed June 15, 2012).

20. According to a 2010 survey conducted by The Center for the Constitution at James Madison's Montpelier, 34 percent of Americans responded that the Constitution affects their lives on a day-to-day basis only "some," "a little," or "not much." See "The State of the Constitution: What Americans Know," released September 2010.

21. Michigan Department of Education, "What Research Says About Parent Involvement in Children's Education," March 2002, available online at www.michigan. gov/documents/Final_Parent_Involvement_Fact_Sheet_14732_7.pdf (accessed July 1, 2012).

22. Ronald Reagan, "Farewell Address to the Nation," January 11, 1989, available online at www.reagan.utexas.edu/archives/speeches/1989/011189i.htm (accessed May 28, 2012).

23. Jared Sparks, ed., *The Writings of George Washington*, 12 vols. (Boston: American Stationers' Company, 1834–1840), 12:4.

24. Thomas Jefferson to Charles Yancey, January 6, 1816, in Paul Leicester Ford, ed., *The Works of Thomas Jefferson*, 12 vols. (New York: G.P. Putnam's Sons, 1904–1905), 11:497.

25. National Commission on Excellence in Education, *A Nation at Risk: The Imperative for Educational Reform* (Cambridge, MA: U.S. Research, 1984).

FIVE

The Peer Bubble

Mark Bauerlein

On this night, in hundreds of thousands of homes and restaurants across America, families will sit down to dinner together, mom and dad or single-parent and grandparent or friend talking about money or work or travel plans, children tussling and smiling, while one or two teenagers stare at a tiny screen in hand, tapping out messages and sending photos to friends. Watch the teen closely. The others interact, but the adolescent fixates on the mini-keyboard. Eyes are intent, the mouth slides from grin to grimace, thumbs never stop. Mom looks over and blurts, "Eat!" and after a quick bite, attention redirected for a half-second, the 16-year-old jumps back to the screen, tuning out the other persons and everything else without pause.

Everyone has noticed the behavior, and it has become so normal and commonplace that one might blithely shrug it off as but another step in the march of technology. What's the big deal? Teenagers have always shunned their elders, and they've also toyed with gadgets and nifty games for decades. Remember comic books, CB radios, and *Asteroids*? Haven't old folks complained about the kids forever, one might add, and haven't thinkers from Socrates to John Ruskin to Ray Bradbury to Neil Postman raised overwrought alarms about the dangers of this and that machinery? Besides, adults love their iPhones, too, and according to Nielsen Research, 12- to 17-year-olds account for less than 10 percent of PC game minutes played, and 50-year-olds log long nights on Facebook as they track down high school chums and sweethearts . . .[1] Why single out youths, and why do it today?

Because the adolescent at the table engrossed in the tool, oblivious to others nearby, signals a devastating, far-reaching advent, something entirely new in the history of the world. Yes, that is no exaggeration. A profound change in human society has transpired right in front of us. It is not the tools themselves that have caused this cataclysm, but what teenagers do with them. For the reality is this: for the first time ever, individuals pass through the teenage years taking nearly all of their aims and norms and values and styles from one another, not from adults. Their minds and senses are suffused with youth input to heretofore impossible degrees. Outfitted with the latest mobile device—three out of four teenagers have one—they make contact with peers anytime/anywhere, be it on the bus, at the beach, or in the bedroom.[2] Nowhere and at no time do they feel out of touch; or rather, wherever and whenever they are out of touch, they feel that they must and can get back in touch. At any time of the day and well into the night, most of their close friends and virtual friends are busy communicating one way or another, and they absolutely must remain in the loop. According to a 2010 report by Pew Research entitled *Teens and Mobile Phones*, "A fairly common practice seems to be sleeping with one's phone under the pillow, so that it will wake the teen if someone is trying to contact them."[3]

Most grown-ups more than 30 years old can't quite realize the impact of digitally assisted, non-stop peer contact. While 15-year-olds live with the words and glances of other 15-year-olds hourly, 45-year-olds don't obsess over what other people the same age think. They remember peer pressure, of course, but that was a while ago. They didn't pack a 4" × 3" × .5" device containing 100 self-portraits and a four-week record of messages. They never conceived of a personal profile page. While they heeded and spread gossip, got together and broke up, kept diaries and photo albums, they were not able to send a spicy image or late-breaking high school news item to 300 classmates with a quick click.

Adults should try to imagine a regular day in the life of an average 15-year-old boy in the United States. After a quick breakfast, he heads out the door to catch the bus or saunter to school. (Only around 3 percent of youths today are home-schooled.) He looks for friends up ahead, and enemies, too. On the bus he packs in with two dozen others his own age or, at most, three years older or younger. Six-and-a-half hours of in-school time follow, 390 minutes of close quarters neatly age-segregated. Students crowd the hallways between classes, arrange in groups of 25 in trigonometry, U.S. history to 1877, English, and biology, disburse into cliques at separate tables in the cafeteria, compete in gym class, then shower and change side by side. Different parts of the building and grounds are claimed as turf by different groups. After the last class ends, he might remain on campus for band or soccer practice, student government or a planning committee, or an hour of detention. If not, he heads to a buddy's basement for two hours of *Halo 3: ODST* and hanging out.[4] He heads home at 5:00 pm and commences the most popular leisure habit of his age group, flipping on the television set and surfing for the right programs.[5] Fortunately for him, he can choose from a rich and relevant array of offerings entirely or partly centered on the real and fantastical experiences of his cohort.

- 16 & Pregnant
- Tyler Perry's House of Payne
- That '70s Show
- The Amazing Spiez!
- The Suite Life on Deck
- Beverly Hills 90210
- *Stand and Deliver* (a 1988 film)
- *The Thirteenth Year* (a 1999 film)
- High School Stories
- *The Freshman* (a 1990 film)[6]

After 90 minutes of viewing, dinner is ready. Perhaps he must undergo a meal with one or two parents, but once again, with the cell phone close by, he can text pals between mouthfuls. After all, kids his age run up 100 texts per day, and they also make around 230 calls per month.[7] Afterwards, from 7:00 pm until lights out, digital exchanges can go on and on, often with the TV running in the background. Yes, there is homework to do, but according to the Spring 2008 High School Survey of Student Engagement (HSSSE), fully 82 percent of high school students complete five hours or less of written homework per week, while 90 percent of them complete five hours or less of reading/studying homework (43 percent do one hour or less of written work, 55 percent do one hour or less of reading/studying). In other words, the odds are that he won't put in even one entire hour of study. Over the same week, we might add, 85 percent of his cohort devotes five hours or less to "Reading for self," reading which, presumably, may include newspapers, *Harry Potter*, *Sin City*, and *ESPN Magazine*. (Fifty-four percent come in at one hour or less.)[8]

That leaves three hours or so for more texting, more uploading of photos of him and his friends, some Facebook updates, and MTV broadcasting continuously. His desk offers so much more than the civics textbook and *The Catcher in the Rye*. Here we see the all-out transformation of the home. With the teenage bedroom equipped with laptop, television set, Blackberry, video game console, and iPod, that upstairs room at the end of the hall is not a secluded space—it's a social clearing.[9] There our 15-year-old can shut out the rest of the home and open multiple lines of outside communication. He winds down and approaches bedtime surrounded by text messages and emails, news about youth celebrities, music favored by his crowd, head shots and homemade videos. And when he finally falls asleep, the rush of teen stuff keeps going, piling up just a few feet away on the cell phone, the Facebook page, and the email account.

This is not an unusual day and night. Girls have a different routine, true, but only slightly. While they do more homework than boys, read more often on their own, and rack up fewer video game minutes, they send more text messages and make more cell phone calls.[10] For both sexes, as research from Nielsen, Pew, Kaiser, HSSSE, MacArthur, and many other private and public sources records again and again, the "always on" presence of digital tools and the concomitant 24/7 nearness of peers form an entirely normal condition. Never have adolescents enjoyed (and suffered) so much access to one another, and the phenomenon has happened oh-so-quickly. Adolescents today don't know any other reality, and so they adapt through the middle school years and learn the mores as a matter of course. Filling time alone with chatting and texting and photo-sharing—that is, converting actual solitude into virtual togetherness—they turn their adolescence into an intense age-confined acculturation. With social life extending beyond the actual mingling of persons, the customary effects of youth culture broaden and deepen. Peer pressure escalates, peer consciousness expands, and so do all the markers of prestige and instruments of conformity. Show up to school with the wrong haircut and the others won't let up for days. Drop a word such as *intractable* or *sincerity* or *reactionary* into lunchroom conversation and people will blink and scowl. Taste amplifies into a competition for "knowing-ness." If our 15-year-old gets caught listening to Frank Sinatra singing "Summer Wind," his reputation plummets. Say something critical about rap music, call it "vulgar bellowing," and he might get punched. Individual interests coalesce around the interests of the group. Such dispositions have reigned among teens for decades, but with digital tools at hand, they crank up to all-encompassing levels.

Meanwhile, the influence of parents and mentors wanes. A day in the life of an average 15-year-old allows only scattered moments of meaningful conversation between them, a few minutes at the breakfast and dinner table, in the car while driving to a game, in the bedroom before retiring. Set dad's input alongside the input of other 15-year-olds and it looks like a molehill beside a mountain.

This is not normal. Or rather, it is normal today, but utterly abnormal at any other time. The logged-on, screen-lit adolescent key-striking to peers and treating adults as background noise appears everywhere, shocking nobody, but in comparison with youths in other eras, one who spends so much time connected to friends and disconnected from adults is a freakish condition. Today, nearly every teenager enters high school. Around 20 to 30 percent of public school students drop out at some point.[11] Of those who remain, approximately two-thirds go directly into a post-secondary institution. This means that most teenagers spend nearly half of their waking hours during the academic year pressed against one another in classrooms, hallways, lunchrooms, and gyms. And for around 50 percent of them, the youth-dominated milieu proceeds for another one or two or more years (more than 40 percent of youths who go straight to a four-year college do not graduate within six years, dropping out somewhere along the way—for two-year colleges, the dropout rate is higher).

Compare those numbers to previous times. Back in 1900, only 11 percent of high school-aged persons attended high school. By 1930, the rate had risen tremendously, but it still stood at only 51 percent. In his important 1961 study of the consequences of increased school attendance, *The Adolescent Society*, James Coleman attributed the rise not to progressive notions of spreading secondary education through the middle and working classes, but rather to the general process of industrialization, which demands more technical and specialized skills and knowledge than does an agrarian economy.[12] Whatever the causes, the generational impact is clear. Before, kids left school after sixth, seventh, or eighth grade, and their destination was the wholly non-youth-oriented world of work. Some went into the factories since child labor laws were slack or nonexistent at the time. Others joined their fathers for work on the farm or mothers for work in the garden, kitchen, and washroom. Still others helped parents who owned a small business, a shop in town or services provided to a community. In each case, parents and bosses regulated their activity. By their late-teens, young Americans had put in years of labor and had assimilated the burdens of adulthood. The hours and habits of teen school and leisure life today would have appeared to them as unreal as the events in *Grimm's Fairy Tales*. It is not simply that there was no television, laptop, or Blackberry. The simple fact of three or four hours a day of real and virtual socializing they could not even imagine. They might have been just as interested in one another, but they did not have the chance to act on it. They had no choice but to take their cues from grown-ups, not peers.

Even their entertainments did not divorce the realm of adolescence from adult pressures. The leading young adult book sensation of the day was the Horatio Alger series. In titles such as *Brave and Bold, or, The Fortunes of a Factory Boy; Paul the Peddler, or, The Fortunes of a Young Street Merchant*; and *Risen from the Ranks, or, Harvey Walton's Success*, plucky and entrepreneurial youths fend off exploitative adults and cooperate with benevolent ones, their hard work and honesty ultimately bringing them success and good will. They are not out to prevail on the athletic field, to acquire fancy gadgets, or to discern the latest youth fads. They don't think much about the esteem of their fellows. They want money and position, both of them earned the old-fashioned way generally on the model of the archetypal American teen story, Ben Franklin, whose best-selling *Autobiography* for 150 years drew a map for young Americans to follow if they wanted to prosper in the New World.

Set the experiences of Franklin and Alger's heroes alongside the adventures of the young adult book-hero sensation today, Harry Potter. Harry has much of the same independence and wit as they do, but he lives in a fantasy world of wizards and powers, most of the action taking place in a school with lots of friends and classmates nearby. Franklin's and Paul the Peddler's triumphs—publishing a newspaper piece, earning a dollar on the streets—are entirely familiar and ordinary in an actual adult setting, and they would impress others just as much if they were achieved by adults. There is no distinction between what an astute 16-year-old aims to accomplish and what a 26-year-old aims to accomplish. Harry's triumphs, however, take place in an unreal adolescent setting—confrontations with evil, the learning of potions, etc.—and one would not respect an adult who engages in the same efforts. Most importantly, while youth friendships and rivalries appear here and there in the older books, they don't possess significant value and the heroes don't mull over their own social status. Harry's peers, on the other hand, both friends and enemies, are critical parts of his life. Yes, the series as a whole does present Harry progressing toward adulthood, but heaps of social stuff fill his career along the way. With Alger and Franklin, adult matters press down on them from the start, and their experience reflects the adult-heavy circumstances of adolescence at the time.

Not only their entertainments, but their leisure training, too, followed the heading of adults. Outlining the difficulties teenage girls endure in the transition to womanhood, psychologist Leonard Sax recalls several crucial but now-forgotten mentoring practices outside the home and common to rural and urban communities alike not so long ago. "I'm not talking only about mothers teaching their daughters," he writes, "but about a community of women teaching girls. We used to have many such communities in the United States, formal and informal: quilting circles, sewing circles, all-female Bible study groups, all-female book groups, Girl Scout troops, the variety of women's clubs that operated in association with the Federation of Women's Clubs and so forth."[13] Sax cites the "bowling alone" thesis of Robert Putnam, that is, the decline of neighborhood activities and civic associations in American society since the mid-twentieth century, one of its consequences being directly relevant to the issue at hand—grown-ups and teenagers having substantial engagement with one another. Sax regards the disengagement of older women from teenage girls as a catastrophe, and like Coleman 50 years earlier, he sees it as a novel advent ("Girls teaching same-age girls what it means to be a woman is a new phenomenon in human history").[14] One hardly needs to point out the deficiencies of 15-year-old girls showing 15-year-old girls how to think and judge and act as a woman.

It cannot be halted, though, not on a broad scale. The extension of schooling to the early twenties and the spread of after-school socializing happened over the course of the twentieth century with all the momentum that money, technology, and media could supply. How many parents kept the television out of the home? How many 16-year-olds skipped *Animal House* and *The Breakfast Club*? How many parents will not let them sidle into The Apple Store? Back in the old days, a thirteenth birthday meant the end of childhood and the introduction to adulthood, sometimes an abrupt and disheartening threshold, but inevitable nonetheless. By 1960, a different transition had arrived, as Coleman summarized: "The adolescent is dumped into a society of his peers, a society whose habitats are the halls and classrooms of the school, the teen-age canteens, the corner drugstore, the automobile, and numerous other gathering places."[15]

As long as the home remained a non- or limited social zone—a couple of friends in the basement for an hour before dinner, a few landline calls, a teen sitcom or two—the adolescent society had a counter-pressure. Teenagers enduring peer pressure elsewhere enjoyed a temporary reprieve, however much the elders around bored and annoyed them. The words and actions of parents and older siblings reminded them that realms larger than 10th Grade did exist, and that events such as Annual Homecoming were short-lived. The bare presence of elders tempered their perspective, helpfully so. Adolescents tend to magnify the import of what comes about in their contacts, to grant the happenings of teen experience a lifelong consequence. They make the episodes of middle school and high school ("In 9th Grade I was friends with A and B—I'm not friends with them any more") into a meaningful plot, already reading the trajectory of their days on earth as momentous and fateful. When applied to the churning and callous swirl of teenage peers, it is a self-destructive habit. Escape from the adolescent society into the non-social home helped curb it.

With the Digital Age upon us, the healthily antagonistic function of the home is over. Peer-to-peer communication reaches all the way into the bedroom, even under the covers with lights out. This means that the adolescent has no down time, for the tribal games proceed without end. They don't need to change clothes, hop on their bicycle, ride to the "teen-age canteen," and wait for others to arrive. They can meet and greet instantly while lounging on their respective family-room couches wearing pajamas. In a word, for the young, the difference between, on the one hand, home at night and, on the other hand, school hallways, the food court at the mall, the softball field, and other gathering places during the day has crumbled. Adolescents are with each other all the time.

This development will, in fact, have a deeper and longer-lasting impact on American society than did the "Generation Gap" of the Sixties. Yes, the Youth Movement back then rejected and denounced the elders, shouted slogans such as "Don't trust anyone under 30!" and indicted "the Establishment" *in toto*. As Norman Mailer put it in his eccentric chronicle of the 1967 march on the Pentagon, *The Armies of the Night*, "Their radicalism was in their hate for the authority."[16] But however much they reviled mom and dad, the "suits," the "phonies," cops, LBJ and Nixon and Reagan (then-governor of California), the military-industrial complex, and various representations of the status quo, they *engaged* them. Or at least their leaders and spokespersons did. Read "The Port Huron Statement," articles in *Ramparts Magazine*, and other expressions of the Movement (even if some of the writers were approaching 30) and you realize that these voices could not stop talking about the old folks! They might define themselves rigidly against the example of the elders, but the conversation continued. It was an antagonistic relationship, but still a substantive one. Today's youths, in contrast, don't hate their parents and they don't disdain prevailing norms. They just bypass them.

What are the results?

Researchers have begun to assess the emotional and cognitive impact of Facebook, text messaging, cell phones, and screens of all kinds over time. Neuroscientist Gary Small and Gigi Vorgan, for example, argue in a recent book that extended screen time by children and teenagers alters their brain development, among other things hindering their interpersonal awareness and empathy.[17] Another neuroscientist, Torkel Klingberg, argues in *The Overflowing Brain* that the information flooding our senses exceeds the brain's capacity to process it, producing various breakdowns in memory and attention.[18] Anecdotal stories on the costs of the super-social lives of students, too, have begun to surface. In April 2010, for instance, a middle school principal in New Jersey sent an email out to every parent asking that they exercise more control over their children's social networking. Take the laptop out of the bedroom and install parental control software, he advised. Indeed, in a fit of exasperation he questioned the whole activity: *"Let me repeat that—there is absolutely, positively no reason for any middle school student to be part of a social networking site! None."*[19] The objection was not based on moral or reactionary motives, but on practicality. In recent months, problems with social media had taken up fully three-quarters of the labor of school counselors. And while concerns about adult predators abounded, the real dangers lay elsewhere: "The threat to your son or daughter from online adult predators is insignificant compared to the damage that children at this age constantly and repeatedly do to one another through social networking sites or through text and picture messaging."[20]

We do not fully understand the emotional and cognitive outcomes of long-term digital activities by the young, of course, in part because so many of these practices have developed in but a few years' time. Facebook, for instance, just started in 2005, and text messaging exploded only since the mid-2000s. Their full effect will not unfold for several years more, once kids who began using them at age ten reach age 25. By that time, surely, other digital diversions will have surfaced, and they, too, will have more or less delayed effects. We can, however, consider one intellectual outcome of digital tools and the all-peers-all-the-time lifestyle they enable. It is the sharp and firm division of academic matters and leisure interests. When youth culture and peer contact inundate their out-of-school hours so thoroughly, when adult issues infiltrate their leisure time so meagerly, and when those words and sounds and images they share contain so much present-focused, teen-bound content, the materials of the classroom and of intellectual life in general have no personal value, no relevant meaning. What they learn about the First Amendment in civics class and what they see in the op-ed page of their parents' newspaper strike them as an alien planet. Home base is friends and Facebook and *Friends* (30-year-olds acting like 18-year-olds). The content of each realm does not overlap at all. What they talk about with parents and teachers rarely echoes what they talk about with one another.

As a result, academic knowledge has no place in their biographies, at least not during the adolescent chapters. They study the First Amendment in order to take a test, write a paper, and earn a grade, not to become responsible citizens. They read *Walden* because it's on the syllabus. They don't take it to heart as a primer in how to live an independent life and resist the blandishments of money and good repute. Indeed, reading in general has little or minor importance for the majority of teenagers. On the 2008 HSSSE, when asked about the importance of "Reading for self," 18 percent answered "Not at All," 29 percent answered "A Little," and 31 percent answered "Somewhat Important." That left a meager 22 percent to rate it "Very Important" or higher. On the 2007 *National Freshman Attitudes Report*, a study by Noel-Levitz of young people entering college, similarly abysmal findings regarding the personal value of books and reading surfaced.[21] When presented with the statement "Books have never gotten me very excited," 39.6 percent of the 97,000 respondents agreed. Furthermore, 40.4 percent of them admitted, "I don't enjoy reading serious books and articles, and I only do it when I have to." Note, too, that these respondents were the better high school students, the ones heading to college. That so many of them display so little interest in reading, that they possess little intellectual curiosity about matters beyond their personal experience, indicates their priorities. They do want to succeed in school; fully 88.8 percent agreed with the statement, "I am deeply committed to my educational goals, and I'm fully prepared to make the effort and sacrifices that will be needed to attain them." But all-too-many of them don't see any connection between in-school achievement and out-of-school concerns.

This division has its learning effects. People wonder why test results in areas of liberal arts knowledge are so low, for example, why every time the National Assessment of Educational Progress (NAEP) administers the U.S. history exam more than half of twelfth graders score "Below basic."[22] It cannot be attributed to lower intelligence or ambition, for more students go to college than ever before and Advanced Placement course enrollments continue to rise every year. The problem lies in attitudes toward the material. The items on the syllabus do not mean anything to them outside of school, and when knowledge has no personal value, it suffers a natural fate. Once the test is taken, the paper is submitted, and the course ends, the knowledge dissipates. Why retain it if it has served its purpose?

The point is that when teen social life dominates, nay, tyrannizes, the eyes and ears and voices and fingers of youths in leisure hours, the mind drifts away from intellectual pursuits. Reading a book, reading a newspaper, visiting a museum or a library or a gallery, watching C-SPAN, spending time with folks 20 years older . . . such things foster larger perspectives and reinforce academic studies, but they don't reinforce popularity and peer belonging. Teens have never been much inclined to think about history, literature, civics, ethics, and fine art, to be sure, and youth culture has exercised a stiff drag on their attention for decades. Remember the term, for it is not "peer attraction," but "peer pressure." This is why a limit to youth culture is so important to maturity. A little adult pressure is necessary to counter peer pressure, hauling youths to the bookstore, forcing them into the car for a visit to a historic site, keeping the television on CNN and FoxNews, not Nickelodeon. When children have digital tools in hand, adult pressure cannot compete against peer pressure, and the containment of and disregard for academic stuff settles into an everyday youth disposition. This is the catastrophe of the Digital Age, the dark side to all of the marvels and efficiencies Google, Wikipedia, email, and Facebook have provided. The Revolution promised to open minds to more knowledge and information than ever before, to link every tool-equipped individual to the universe of truth and beauty and good. For many people that sublime expansion has indeed taken place, but not for the young ones. The opposite has happened. The cell phone and laptop have, instead, confined them ever more bindingly to the parochial, narrow-minded, anti-intellectual circuit of one another.

NOTES

1. For game minutes played, see *How Teens Use Media: A Nielsen Report on the Myths and Realities of Teen Media Trends* (Nielsen Co., June 2009), 11. The report is available online at blog.nielsen.com/nielsenwire/reports/nielsen_howteensusemedia_june09.pdf. Nielsen's report adopts precisely the "So what?" attitude toward digital media consumption by the young. It opens, in fact, begins, by casting deep concerns about youth and media in pathological terms. "Ephebephobia is the irrational fear of youth," we read, "rooted in the Greek 'ephebos' for youth, and 'phobos' for, well, phobia. While the term was coined just 15 years ago, a curiosity and mystique around youth and their behavior has long been a cultural obsession." Needless to say, *phobia* and *obsession* don't allow for a rational worry over youth habits.

2. A 2008 Harris Interactive poll, *A Generation Unplugged* (available online at files.ctia.org/pdf/HI_TeenMobileStudy_ResearchReport.pdf), found that 79 percent of 13- to 19-year-olds own a mobile device of some kind. A report a year later by Harris Interactive stated that 30 percent of 8- to 12-year-olds own a cell phone (see the results in *Trends & Tudes*, vol. 8, December 2009, available online at www.harrisinteractive.com/vault/HI_TrendsTudes_2009_v08_i04.pdf).

3. See Amanda Lenhart et al., *Teens and Mobile Phones: Text Messaging Explodes as Teens Embrace It as the Centerpiece of Their Communication Strategies with Friends*, a report by Pew Internet & American Life Project (April 20, 2010), available online www. pewinternet.org/~/media//Files/Reports/2010/PIP-Teens-and-Mobile-2010.pdf.

4. For video game playing by teenagers, see Amanda Lenhart et al., *Teens, Video Games, and Civics: Teens' Gaming Experiences Are Diverse and Include Significant Social Interaction and Civic Engagement*, a report by Pew Internet & American Life Project, supported by MacArthur Foundation (September 16, 2008), available online at www. macfound.org/atf/cf/%7BB0386CE3-8B29-4162-8098-E466FB856794%7D/PEW_DML_REPORT_080916.PDF. Researchers found that 97 percent of 12- to 17-year-olds play games on one or another digital device, while 50 percent of them played games the previous day.

5. According to the Kaiser Foundation, 71 percent of 8- to 18-year-olds have a television set in their bedrooms, and they spend four hours and 29 minutes watching "television content" in their own rooms or elsewhere. See *Generation M²: Media in the Lives of 8- to 18-Year-Olds* (January 2010), available online at www.kff.org/entmedia/upload/8010.pdf. Nielsen counts teenagers at three hours and 20 minutes per day watching television (see *How Teens Use Media*).

6. These listings come from Comcast Cable in Atlanta for Friday, May 14, 2010. They do not include abundant teen-oriented programs available through "On Demand" selections, such as shows on the Disney Channel.

7. On its *nielsenwire* blog on September 22, 2008 (available online at blog.nielsen. com/nielsenwire/online_mobile/in-us-text-messaging-tops-mobile-phone-calling/), Nielsen reported that 13- to 17-year-olds who have a mobile phone make 231 calls per month, while 18- to 24-year-olds make 265 calls.

8. See Ethan Yazzie-Mintz, *Engaging the Voices of Students: A Report on the 2007 & 2008 High School Survey of Student Engagement* (Center for Evaluation and Education Policy report, available online at ceep.indiana.edu/hssse/images/HSSSE_2009_Report. pdf). While one chart in the report tabulates hours of time spent on homework and other activities, another chart measures how much importance high school students place on those activities. There, while 29 percent of students in Spring 2008 assigned "Very important" to "Reading/studying for class" and 8 percent gave it "Top priority," "Socializing with friends outside of school" beat reading and studying by a long shot, 43 percent of them rating it "Very important" and 21 percent giving it "Top priority."

9. Kaiser Foundation reports that 75 percent of 8- to 18-year-olds have a radio in the bedroom, 71 percent of them a television set, 68 percent a CD player, 57 percent a DVD or VCR player, 33 percent have Internet access, and 50 percent a video game console. See *Generation M²*.

10. Pew's report on *Teens and Mobile Phones* concluded that "girls are more likely than boys to use both text messaging and voice calling and are likely to do each more frequently" (quotation from p. 6).

11. Because of reporting complications, exact numbers vary from study to study. For one calculation, see Robert Stillwell, *Public School Graduates and Dropouts from the Common Core of Data: School Year 2006-07* (National Center for Education Statistics, October 2009), available online at nces.ed.gov/pubs2010/2010313.pdf.

12. James Coleman, *The Adolescent Society: The Social Life of the Teenager and Its Impact on Education* (New York: Free Press, 1961).

13. Leonard Sax, *Girls on the Edge: The Four Factors Driving the New Crisis for Girls: Sexual Identity, the Cyberbubble, Obsessions, Environmental Toxins* (New York: Basic Books, 2010), 205–6.

14. Sax, *Girls on the Edge*, 206.

15. Coleman, *Adolescent Society*, 4.

16. Norman Mailer, *The Armies of the Night: History as a Novel, The Novel as History* (New York: New American Library, 1968), 103.

17. Gary Small and Gigi Vorgan, *iBrain: Surviving the Technological Alteration of the Modern Mind* (New York: William Morrow, 2008).

18. Torkel Klingberg, *The Overflowing Brain: Information Overload and the Limits of Working Memory* (New York: Oxford University Press, 2008).

19. The principal's name is Anthony Orsini of Bergen County Middle School. Portions of his letter are available online at thevillageofridgewood.com/anthony-orsini-benjamin-franklin-middle-school-asks-parents-to-ban-social-networking-sites/ (accessed June 15, 2012).

20. See Jason Kessler, "Principal to Parents: Take Kids off Facebook," April 30, 2010, available online at articles.cnn.com/2010-04-30/tech/principal.facebook.ban_1_social-networking-social-networking-site-facebook (accessed May 29, 2012).

21. Noel-Levitz, *National Freshman Attitudes Report* (2007), available online at https://www.noellevitz.com/NR/rdonlyres/3934DA20-2C31-4336-962B-A1D1E7731D8B/0/2007FreshmanAttitudes.pdf.

22. For NAEP test scores in U.S. History in years 1994, 2001, and 2006 for Grades 4, 8, and 12, see nationsreportcard.gov/ushistory_2006/ (accessed June 15, 2012). One can also probe the data to determine how students scored on each particular question. For example, on the 2006 exam, when asked in short-answer format for "One Reason Why U.S. in Korean War," only 14 percent provided an "Appropriate" response. More than one-third of them couldn't identify the reason behind the 1962 U.S.-Soviet "conflict." Scores on the NAEP civics exams aren't much better. On the 2006 assessment, only 27 percent of twelfth-graders scored "Proficient" or "Advanced." See nationsreportcard.gov/civics_2006/c0103.asp?tab_id=tab3&subtab_id=Tab_1–chart (accessed June 15, 2012).

SIX

Voter Beware

Responsible Voting in an Age of Political Marketing

Lisa Spiller and Jeff Bergner

What does it mean to be a responsible voter? What must voters know to cast their ballots in an intelligent way? Much of the literature on this topic decries the absence of voters' basic historical and political knowledge as well as their lack of substantive knowledge of individual candidates. Typical American voters are unfamiliar with the basics of the American electoral system and with the history that has shaped political life and ideals. Indeed, the shortcomings of contemporary civic education as well as the ambivalence regarding its worth have been well noted in other chapters of this volume.

This chapter focuses on a second challenge to responsible voting. Political campaigns today are more sophisticated than ever, employing marketing and communication tools in sly new ways to shape voters' opinions on issues as well as their impressions of candidates. This newly emerging consumer-centered political marketing has raised the bar to responsible voting to new levels. Not only are most voters devoid of general political and historical knowledge, they are also being manipulated by candidates who employ marketing techniques in unforeseen and radical new ways to shape voters' perceptions and desires. This chapter will analyze the marketing weapons that will be henceforth used in political campaigns to assist American voters who wish to be civically responsible. Though political marketing is not altogether new, we show not only that candidates' marketing tools and techniques are novel, but that

America's electoral process lacks the features that have previously moderated their use.

CAMPAIGNING IN AMERICA

Haven't American politicians—since the very first federal elections in 1789—always campaigned for office by skillfully creating a public persona? Haven't candidates always shaped and shaded their views, taking care to stress what they believed would be persuasive and well received by voters? In short, hasn't political marketing always been a feature of American politics?

It is true that American politicians, not only self-interested rogues, have from the earliest days of the republic maneuvered behind the scenes to secure electoral support. No less a figure than the father of the Constitution, James Madison, actively advanced his own interests. Madison found himself temporarily shut out of representing Virginia in the new Senate which he did so much to create. As a result, he conducted numerous hidden meetings to secure election to the House of Representatives. American politicians were never as pure or innocent as they pretended to be in public.[1]

However, a healthy public ethos moderated the political process in the early republic; there was a public prejudice against men who seemed too eager to serve in political office. To be labeled politically ambitious was no praise for the classically educated gentlemen who dominated American political life at the end of the eighteenth century. In that regard, the proper stance for a candidate was to "stand," not to "run" for office, which meant that candidates had to feign reluctance to serve, and only to serve by answering a "call" to do so.[2] As well-known political commentator Hugh Heclo has aptly stated, "For a long time, respectable opinion remained disdainful of the idea of a politician's strenuously seeking to persuade people to vote for him. Would someone whose character was not already known and who had to sell himself really be fit for public office? Should one entrust power to someone who courted public favor?"[3] Thus, the very idea of overt political marketing was traditionally rejected by public sentiment.

America's electoral politics have obviously come a long way from the mindset that would pose such questions. The process by which this has occurred in American history has been gradual, but there have been notable mileposts along the way.

THE POLITICAL PARTY SYSTEM

The first milepost was the development of the political party system in America. The Constitution's framers were wary of political parties, seeing them as the embodiment of "faction." Accordingly, there was no place in their thinking for the existence of relatively fixed political parties. But it did not take long for such parties to emerge. This had both pleasant and unpleasant consequences. On the positive side, standing political parties suggested that it was not treasonous to oppose the government's policies; opposition was to be expected, so long as the political opposition operated within relatively vague but fixed bounds. Competing political viewpoints seemed a fair and reasonable outcome; the idea of a "loyal opposition" eventually took hold in America.

Political parties organized themselves to choose and actively support their candidates and to oppose those of the other party. So far from the idea of candidates demurely "standing" for office, political parties created an apparatus to advance the prospects of their chosen candidates. Political campaigns emerged, the word "campaign" itself revealing the changes which were occurring in the American political landscape. This is a military term, borrowed from the description of a plan to do battle with the other side. Just like armies, political parties went out into the "field" to wage campaigns against their opponents.[4] Political parties did not just advance the interests of their own candidates; they actively and often scurrilously attacked candidates of the opposing party. Newspapers affiliated with political parties became the favored instruments of personal and ideological attacks on opponents. Negative campaigning was often practiced with a ferocity that makes today's negative campaigns seem pale by comparison.

Political parties, especially in American urban centers, fueled corruption on a widespread scale. Party bosses, who often bought votes from newly arrived immigrants, consolidated their hold on the political process. Bosses chose the candidates who were then beholden to the bosses, as were the voters whose loyalty had been purchased by political favors.

In the late nineteenth and early twentieth centuries, the populist and progressive movements targeted political party machines just like they went after large corporations.[5] Populists advanced a number of political reforms designed to break the power of political machines and to bring candidates and voters closer together. One of the most significant reforms, the Seventeenth Amendment to the Constitution, provided for the direct election of U.S. senators. No longer would senators be hand-picked by party bosses and their acolytes in the state legislatures.

Populist reformers also sought to weaken party bosses by increasing opportunities for direct participation and by expanding the electorate. They created procedures for issue referendums and for the recall of elected officials to allow the electorate to express its will directly. They furthermore aimed to weaken party bosses by bringing new voters into the fold. Chief among these efforts was the adoption of the Nineteenth Amendment, guaranteeing women the right to vote. This spirit of reform was reflected by the populist candidate for president, William Jennings

Bryan. In 1896, he toured the country speaking on his own behalf at rallies and political gatherings 600 times, reaching five million people in 27 states.[6]

TECHNOLOGICAL ADVANCES

New technologies made further changes in political campaigning possible by bringing candidates closer to the public. Prior to the twentieth century, few Americans had ever heard the voice or seen the visage of a president or presidential contender. With the advent of radio, Americans could hear the voice of their leaders, and of their candidates, and could draw their own direct impressions about these candidates. Radio became an increasingly important political medium in the 1920s, and in 1928 Republicans dedicated the major part of their publicity budget to radio.[7] Franklin D. Roosevelt explored radio's full potential by issuing "Fireside Chats," which enabled him to enter living rooms across America on a weekly basis. Radio also broadcast political conventions, which ushered in an era of direct participation in conventions by presidential nominees. Franklin Roosevelt broadened his direct bond with citizens by becoming the first presidential nominee to appear in-person at his party's convention to claim the nomination.

Television took the personal connection with candidates to a new level by amplifying voters' sense of direct knowledge of the candidates. Although television spots aired in the 1948, 1952, and 1956 campaigns, the 1960 presidential debates between Richard Nixon and John F. Kennedy displayed the full force of television's power to sway elections. Television remains the leading medium for candidates to reach American voters to this day, through coverage of presidential debates, paid campaign advertisements, and general news stories.

The combined effects of television and radio permitted and encouraged a fundamental shift in the American political landscape that would forever weaken the hold that party bosses had over candidates: the modern political primary. After World War II, greater numbers of states and localities adopted a primary election system in lieu of nomination by political party leaders. As long as party leaders controlled the nomination process, they exercised a good degree of control over both the electoral process and the kinds of candidates who would serve in office. The nearly universal political primary nominating process empowers candidates to self-select. No longer beholden in any significant way to party leaders, successful candidates now often choose the party leaders. This shift also isolates the individual political candidate to a degree. To be a candidate for federal office today means to compete aggressively, more or less on one's own, from day one of the primary process straight through the general election.

We are now in the midst of another technological revolution. The computer revolution—and the Internet with its wide variety of platforms—promises to transform the electoral process by offering candidates new and potent ways to communicate with, shape opinions of, and raise money from potential voters. Every election since 1992 has witnessed—and, we believe, every future election will witness—a growing role for computer-related campaign activities. We do not yet know the full force of the Internet's power. The last two decades of elections have uncovered a range of possibilities in identifying candidates, allowing new and previously unknown candidates to emerge, segmenting the market in ever more refined ways, mobilizing voter turnout, and raising campaign funds, all of which are likely to continue to change the face of the modern campaign.

SCIENTIFIC POLLING AND MESSAGE DEVELOPMENT

Another significant development occurred with the advent of business marketing tools in political campaigns. These tools—which Hugh Heclo calls "political technologies"—included a new and systematic focus on "public relations." The development of an innovative technique, scientific polling, made new public relations/marketing activities possible and effective. Polling produced information that was inherently interesting and that constituted a kind of "news" about where issues or candidates stood in the minds of the American people at a particular moment in time. Polling also proved useful for candidates who sought to portray themselves as the "inevitable" choice, thus creating a bandwagon effect to fulfill the prophecy. But the most significant use of scientific polling was actually instituted by marketers rather than the candidates themselves, to develop messages that would appeal to voters. Polling is now used to discover what does and does not appeal to voters (who are, in fact, political consumers). In short, polling made possible meaningful testing of different ways to present the same product (i.e., issue or candidate) to the public.

Scientific polling and message development has become increasingly sophisticated over the past five decades, but even in 1967 the politically astute team which surrounded Richard Nixon was well aware of their power. As Nixon speechwriter Raymond Price later recalled:

> Let's leave realities aside—because what we have to deal with now is not the facts of history, but an image of history. . . . We have to be very clear on this point; that the response is to the image, not to the man, since 99% of the voters have no contact with the man. It's not what's there that counts, it's what's projected—and, carrying it one step further, it's not what he projects but rather what the voter receives. . . . We have to bear constantly in mind that it's not what we say that counts,

but what the listener hears; not what we project, but how the viewer receives the impression.[8]

The next three decades of presidential campaigns elaborated upon these insights. The Reagan campaigns brought a sophisticated California TV media operation to Washington, while the Clinton campaign introduced the "war room" to guarantee rapid responses to breaking news and especially to opposition attacks. George W. Bush's campaigns of 2000 and 2004 broadened these techniques by "micro-targeting" specific audiences for tailored messages. Micro-targeting involves the collection of hundreds of data points, such as voter information, lifestyle information, family composition, financial data, geographic data, political interests, attitudes and opinions to group voters into specific niches. Once separated into groups, the marketer, or candidate, can develop precise ways to reach and interact with them.

MARKETING TECHNIQUES AND THE 2008 OBAMA CAMPAIGN

The Obama presidential campaign of 2008 took political campaigning to a new level of sophistication by employing consumer-based marketing strategies, including product branding, mass customization, and micro-targeting to sell a created persona. When campaigning for Richard Nixon, Raymond Price understood a well-run campaign to be one which presented images of reality as favorably as possible. This was an understandable approach. Nixon, after all, was a very well-known commodity in 1968—having been a prominent congressman during the McCarthy Era, vice president under Dwight Eisenhower, the Republican nominee for president in 1960, and a candidate for governor of California in 1962.

The 2008 Obama presidential campaign, by contrast, had no such fixed reality binding it. The American public did not know who Barack Obama was, and the media did not unearth or communicate many details about his life. The Obama campaign wisely turned his not-being-known into a virtue by extending the use of marketing techniques that first took form in the 1960s. The Obama campaign thus completely inverted the political marketing task. Instead of following the traditional method of creating a favorable image of reality and then selling that image to the public, Obama's team followed contemporary marketing theory by *beginning with what people want and shaping the image of the candidate to fit these desires*. Thus, with the 2008 Obama campaign, we have moved beyond a product-centric marketing strategy to a customer-centered approach. The creation of candidate Obama was therefore much like a company's creation of a product. His team achieved its goals by understanding the needs and wants of its consumers and fulfilling their expressed desires better than any of its competitors.

BRANDING THE CANDIDATE

Obama's team masterfully branded candidate Obama. In customer-centered political marketing, the "brand" cannot be successfully established separate and apart from the needs and wants of the American electorate; it must grow out of them. In marketing, the brand is the persona that envelops a product, organization, or person. It makes a promise to the buyer (or in the case of a political candidate, the voter) that the product or person will carry traits for which the brand is known. Although product branding has been around for a long time, the concept of personal branding—branding you as a person—has not been widely employed until the last decade or so. Political candidates who run for office attempt to convey to voters a brand image to persuade them to cast their votes for him or her.

The marketing process begins with understanding the consumer, or the voter, not with the candidate and a set of pre-established positions on the issues. Similarly, the political candidate's task begins with the needs and desires of the electorate and creating the candidate from the ground up, as it were, to respond to these very needs and wants. In fact, the first stage of the marketing process has nothing to do with the product, or, in this case, the candidate and his views. The notion of candidates trying to persuade people of the truth of their own (deeply held) beliefs is foreign to modern political marketing campaigns. Candidates now focus on creating the brand that best resonates with the voters' preferences, whatever they may be. The brand will take on the identity that aligns most closely to the desires of the target consumer. Once again, consumer research is driving the marketing strategy—in this case, brand creation. This is the same process by which any product, service, organization, or political candidate develops a brand. First comes research to understand the desires of the target market. Then, and only then, is that information used to create a persona or image of the object or person being branded. Once established, brands take on a unique *brand personality*, which is a set of human characteristics associated with a brand.[9] Of course, products, services, and organizations are innate objects. When branding an innate object, the marketer strategically strives to give the object a human personality so it will emotionally connect with its audience. This is not the case when branding people. The challenge in political marketing lies in incorporating the candidate's own personality traits, building on desirable traits and downplaying undesirable ones, and creating a brand that will consistently embody the image the candidate wishes to leave in the voter's mind.

Branding is the umbrella under which all of the elements of a brand are clustered. It is the simple, yet comprehensive expression of one broad truth which a candidate wants to express. Branding may be comprised of words, images, sounds, or personified objects or characters. Regardless of the elements used to brand a given product, service, organization, or person, all of the branding elements must be used in a consistent manner. Consistency is the key.

In addition, the brand must also be "new" or unique to be effective. The purpose of a brand is to help products, organizations, or people stand out and be distinguished from others. Most political candidates have not gone to great lengths to create innovative logos to brand their candidacies. Obama was the exception to this rule. His logo took on a unique shape—a free-flowing "O" as opposed to the typical rectangular or square box. Finally, in a campaign, the brand must become the *big idea* or center of the entire marketing campaign. In marketing the "big idea" is sometimes referred to as the *meme*, a term coined by Richard Dawkins in 1976 and later applied to marketing by Jay Conrad Levinson in his book *Guerrilla Creativity*. A meme is the essence of an idea, expressed as a symbol or set of words, an action or a sound—or all of these.[10] According to Obama campaign design director Scott Thomas:

> The true reason that Obama's logo and design work were so powerful [was] consistency and a carefully cultivated brand message that effectively captured the spirit of hope, change and action [that] made the campaign's identity extremely powerful. Every time a voter interacted with a piece of the campaign's brand, whether it was a sign, button, or social network profile, they were greeted by familiar design elements that they recognized and identified with.[11]

In other words, the Obama team successfully combined newness in the logo, a simple "big idea" that resonated with voters, and consistency in the delivery of their message. One can only surmise that future savvy politicians will learn from the Obama example and work to emulate these successful methods.

DATABASE-DRIVEN POLITICAL MARKETING

Not only do modern consumer-centric political campaigns like Obama's tell voters what they want to hear and brand themselves accordingly, they do so in ever more carefully targeted, personalized, and individualized ways. This process of connecting with voters is called "mass customization," and it was developed to its fullest point yet by the 2008 Obama campaign team. Mass customization entails tailoring campaign messages to the unique preferences of individual voters on a high-volume scale.[12]

Most political campaigns begin by analyzing voting data accumulated from the past several elections to identify the strongest and weakest performing districts and the demographics for the prospective political party. Voter registration lists help candidates identify precincts in which past candidates have performed as well, worse, or better than expected. Voter registration drives can then focus on specific market segments, such as young voters, which tend to have lower voter registration rates and thus lower voter turnout rates.[13] The Obama campaign team worked magic on this task for both the primary and general election campaigns. In Iowa, for example, campaign manager David Plouffe declared: "We had to grow the share of the electorate we believed would be most supportive of Obama."[14] The 2008 caucuses would have to be younger, attended by more minorities, and have a higher percentage of independents and Republicans participating than had historically been the case. And the Obama campaign excelled in capturing a far larger share of first-time voters, youth included. First-time voters included a larger than ever share of voters under 30, minority and Hispanic voters.[15]

Campaigns use voting lists as working campaign databases to locate supporters, recruit volunteers, obtain donations, and energize people to vote on election day. In the last few decades, direct marketers have perfected the use of lists and databases to target unique messages to different market segments of consumers. Today, savvy political candidates are employing precise database-driven market segmentation as they campaign for votes.

The customer database (in this case, the voter database) is the vehicle through which a political candidate and his or her team documents comprehensive information about each voter.[16] Beyond a voter's name and address, this information may include geographic, demographic, psychographic, and behavioral data. Armed with personal information about each voter, candidates can effectively craft unique offers, in the form of campaign promises, and disseminate campaign information to gain voter support. One might think of this like a business—because it is.

According to David Plouffe, the Obama campaign began essentially as a start-up business which had nothing—no lists, no equipment, no talent pool.[17] This is a bit of an overstatement because Obama had actually begun building a voter database well before he was a candidate for president. Early in 2006, Obama reached out to political consultant Anita Dunn to help revamp Hopefund, Obama's political action committee (PAC). Hopefund had raised a good amount of money in 2005 but had a small email list of donors.[18] One of Dunn's strategies involved a plan to quickly boost Obama's email list. It was simple: every time Obama spoke at an event for a fellow Democratic candidate, Hopefund would require the host of the event to submit the attendees' email addresses to the PAC.[19] This clever and effective method enabled Obama's team to swiftly build a vast voter database. As financial and other support for Obama's campaign began to pour in, each donor—regardless of donation size—was added to Obama's database. Each donor was motivated to join Obama's organized community of supporters to promote his candidacy. The Obama database reflected the diversity of America—including teachers, retirees, small-business owners, farmers, and students.[20] The Obama campaign team used SMS (short message service) text messages to target its database further by region and to expand its database. Obama offered incentives such as free campaign gear, including buttons and bumper stickers, for those voters who signed up to the campaign's text messaging list. Obama also effectively used campaign rallies to increase the SMS database.[21]

Obama's campaign may have started with a relatively small database, comprised mainly of the names and email addresses of Americans who heard him speak on behalf of other Democratic candidates—but it ended up in November 2008 as a sophisticated database of 13 million supporters. For comparison's sake, this is a decent size broadcasting network.

The Obama team employed dozens of young high-tech digital gurus to shape its database to conduct targeted marketing activities. He began his campaign with a strong database foundation and wisely secured the help of an army of highly talented, computer-savvy volunteers and staff members including the co-founder of Facebook, Chris Hughes, to conduct a powerful database-driven political marketing campaign. Obama's team then customized divergent campaign messages which were designed to target diverse segments of the electorate.

Since the messages of political candidates can now be personalized and delivered to individual voters on a one-to-one basis via email, micro-targeting and mass customization have become powerful tools for political candidates to use in conjunction with their voter database.[22] The Obama campaign team implemented mass customization at every turn via its email database. Obama effectively used his database to motivate campaign supporters and grow his volunteer list. The database was a crucial factor in Obama's ability to connect with American voters.

INDIVIDUALLY TARGETED ONLINE FUNDRAISING

Moreover, Obama's team used micro-targeting and mass customization techniques to raise an unprecedented amount of money online. By September of 2012, more than 3.1 million people had contributed to the Obama campaign. These donors were repeatedly contacted by the campaign, asking for additional contributions. The ease of online contributing—sometimes through regular contributions akin to a payroll deduction plan—facilitated that process. But so did targeted pitches for money. Scarcely a political event could occur—such as Republican nominee John McCain's selection of Sarah Palin as his running mate, a new poll, national economic catastrophe, whatever—without becoming the basis for a new outreach to online contributors. Follow-up after an Obama rally, where thousands of new email addresses were obtained, was a particularly fruitful source of online contributions. Email funding pitches were occasionally sent to the entire list, but more frequently they targeted particular geographical or demographic constituencies.

Further, the Obama team successfully utilized a new fundraising technique—*online* contribution bundling. Contribution bundling, in which well-connected individuals solicit funds from family members, acquaintances, and business colleagues, is not new. The Internet, however, expanded this practice in 2008. Online bundlers solicited one-time or repeat contributions from their acquaintances. Successful bundlers received various rewards ranging from simple "thank yous," to dinner with the candidate.

The Obama campaign reveals a myriad of advantages to online fundraising and bundling:

- requests and responses are rapid
- easier for the donor
- can be coordinated from a single location
- allows a campaign to reach highly targeted lists with a keystroke of the computer
- gives contributors the impression that they are actively involved in the campaign
- minimizes the candidate's investment of personal fundraising time

For these reasons, voters can expect future candidates to utilize this marketing strategy.

POLITICAL CONSUMER BEWARE

In business marketing, certain norms are embodied in contract law or tort law. Coupled with settled precedents and practices, these offer consumers some degree of protection. Better Business Bureau and the fear of bad publicity also shape the practices of many businesses. The states and the federal government maintain regulatory agencies which oversee business practices. In short, there are numerous protections for consumers built into the commercial system. These of course do not guarantee that consumers will not be taken advantage of, and unscrupulous businesses exist in every sector of the commercial world. But there are both upfront legal protections and processes of legal remedy which provide an umbrella of protection for business consumers.

Over and above voluntary business return policies, federal, state, and local governments have established a labyrinth of rules and regulations relating to "claims" that businesses make about their products or services. The Food and Drug Administration (FDA) is perhaps the best known, but by no means the only example of this, overseeing product claims made by the food and pharmaceutical industries. The Department of Agriculture, the Federal Trade Commission, and the Securities and Exchange Commission are all in the business of reviewing the claims made by American businesses for their products. Indeed, there is not a cabinet department or federal regulatory agency that does not engage in this activity. Moreover, courtrooms across America regularly render large dollar judgments on behalf of Americans who have allegedly been taken "unfair advantage" of by business advertising claims. Tobacco companies, to name the best example, even today are being taken to court over their claims—as if there is an American adult with an IQ over 40 who has not known since the 1950s that smoking causes cancer.

What about the "claims" made by political candidates? There are no guarantees or warranties that come with political claims. There is no official organization—neither the Federal Election Commission (FEC) nor any other—that monitors political claims and protects consumers against false or misleading claims.

It is in the modern American political campaign that American voters/consumers have the least protection of all. In politics it is "buyer beware," pure and simple. Candidates can promise whatever they please, and there is no immediate recourse. No one can recover "damages" from a candidate who misleads voters with false claims. For that matter, candidates—or political leaders—can make claims that are not only false, but completely meaningless and impossible in principle to measure ("I have saved three million jobs") and there is no recourse comparable to that which exists for false or meaningless claim-making in the business world.

National level politics is regulated—if that is the right word—solely by the FEC. All charges made against candidates and their campaigns are funneled through this regulatory body. But the FEC has been established by the very politicians it is supposed to oversee, and it has been deliberately created to be a toothless organization. The principal role of the FEC is to receive and monitor financial information which is provided by candidates. The FEC does not collect information on its own, but relies on what it is provided by candidates. This information is made public on the FEC's website. In this regard, the FEC serves more as a clearinghouse than a regulatory body.

The FEC does have legal authority to investigate instances of alleged improper campaign fundraising and to levy fines against candidates' campaigns. But the force of this authority is blunted in two ways. First, FEC commissioners are carefully balanced between the two major political parties. Neither party has an independent set of incentives to be overly investigative; what is sauce for the goose is sauce for the gander. Unlike other government or quasi-government entities—which regulate activities to which they have no formal connection—FEC commissioners regulate the campaigns of the political parties to which they quite openly and explicitly belong.

Second, as a practical matter the FEC has virtually no ability to affect candidates' actions during the political campaign itself. Campaign fundraising violations are often difficult to detect, and require sorting through mountains of data. As a result, if the FEC pursues an alleged violation of campaign finance laws, it occurs long after the campaign has ended and the election has taken place. One example serves to make this point. In July 2010, the FEC found that Joe Biden's 2008 presidential campaign had accepted excessive financial contributions, and ordered the Biden campaign to pay $219,000 to the Treasury to resolve these issues. This ruling occurred a full two years after the incident and nearly two years after the Biden campaign had ended. This FEC decision was predictably buried in a small article in the back pages of American newspapers, if run at all.

If FEC regulation of campaigns' finances is weak generally, it is nearly non-existent with regard to the increasingly important role of Internet fundraising. The federal government has until recently been cautious about regulating the Internet and political uses of the Internet are no exception. The 2006 FEC Internet regulations exempt the Internet from many restrictions of campaign finance laws. The full panoply of campaign Internet activities that can be conducted by individuals all take place outside the limitations and the publicity required for in-kind contributions (time or other indirect forms of assistance which have a monetary value) which occur outside the Internet. It should not be surprising that the FEC has not seriously investigated any of the charges that (because of the ease of contributing to its website for foreign nationals) the Obama campaign received substantial amounts of funds from prohibited foreign sources.

It is sometimes argued that the FEC is not toothless because it has pursued alleged violations of campaign finance law committed by independent expenditure groups, particularly after the 2004 presidential election. This, however, is just what one might expect. Politicians and their acolytes at the FEC will pursue outside groups with far more rigor than either their own candidates' campaigns or their own political parties' fundraising. In like manner, politicians denounce evil "lobbyists" and require elaborate disclosure of their activities, but in no meaningful way restrict lobbyists' contributions to their political campaigns.

This is not an argument in favor of creating a federal body to monitor and evaluate political claims. There is much—far too much—that would be problematic with such a body. A free people should not require a pseudo-objective entity to make judgments about the validity of political claims. Independent minded and educated American citizens should possess the tools to make these judgments themselves. This is precisely the point. The American electorate swings from hope to disappointment, hope to disappointment through successive election cycles. Why should this be so? It is because too much of the electorate all too naively believes what it hears in campaign promise after campaign promise—and hence sets itself up for an inevitable letdown. An electorate that enthuses itself over empty campaign promises like "change" deserves what it gets.

WHAT VOTERS NEED TO KNOW

The 2008 Obama presidential campaign was a state-of-the art campaign the likes of which voters should expect to see in future races. Its branding and strategic focus on message were particularly impressive. How should voters cope with the onslaught of political marketing which comes around regularly? The best run campaigns will be voter-centric, emanating from the voter's hopes and fears. These campaigns will not simply sell voters what they want; they sell voters *exactly* what they want, as revealed through extensive polling and focus group testing.

Candidates can be expected to manipulate voters by over-promising during campaigns, presenting ideal images of themselves, and reinforcing their idealized image through "branding." They will then attach their brand to a big idea, like "change," which voters can interpret however they please.

In the Digital Age campaigns assemble enormous quantities of personal information, some of which is shared freely by the voters themselves, but much of which is collected by the campaigns from databases that contain their home addresses, buying habits, and lifestyle preferences. Candidates now use this information cornucopia to target voters with the precise messages to which they will be most receptive. While candidates utilize a general and recognizable "brand," different voter segments hear customized messages via targeted media channels addressed personally to them about what that candidate's brand can do for them.

Moreover, it is crucial to recognize that the mass media is not a neutral transmitter of information to voters, but reflects its owners' and participants' political preferences. Media outlets are often biased in favor of one or another candidate. Information provided by these outlets can be "fact-checked" and still quite biased. "Information" circulating on the Internet often does not have the merit of even minimal fact-checking. Television entertainment shows which address political topics do not present information in any meaningful sense of the word; they are purely entertainment and "facts" presented on these shows have misled legions of viewers. Voters need to be aware of the source of all political claims, not just those issued by the candidates or their campaigns.

It is especially easy to raise money via targeted online appeals, and individually targeted online fundraising is the wave of the future. Online fundraising is not only easier for both candidates and contributors; it can be personalized to a far greater extent than either direct mail or mass media solicitations. As such, there are far more opportunities to mislead voters into thinking they are receiving personal communications when they are in fact receiving highly targeted individual appeals.

Finally, it is important to note—despite contemporary governance that looks ever more like non-stop campaigning—that governing is *not* the same as campaigning. It is easier to make promises than it is to keep them. It is more difficult for officials to manage their brand while serving in office than while campaigning for office. This is especially true for candidates who make sweeping and unrealistic promises during their campaigns. Voters must stay informed after the campaign to hold their elected officials accountable for broken promises.

CONSUMER-BASED CANDIDATE MARKETING AND THE FUTURE OF AMERICAN DEMOCRACY

Political marketing employs highly sophisticated tools to brand political candidates and influence voters' decisions. Among all types of marketing, only political marketing is largely unregulated. Thus, political claims require a special degree of vigilance.

Numerous ethical issues are raised by the accumulation of personal information and the use of manipulative tactics in political marketing. Some nations have turned to the government itself to regulate political speech, that is, to determine what can and cannot be said and to determine the guidelines for what is "proper" and reasonable political speech. Public financing requirements have taken the United States a first step down this course. Public financing laws do not generally seek to regulate directly the content of political claims, but they do set out to "balance"—and clearly to limit—the financial ability of candidates to make their claims. Those campaign finance laws which aim to prohibit corporations and other entities from certain types of political speech prior to elections are more direct efforts to regulate political speech.

The trend in America today, however, is to move *away* from public financing and from the regulation of political speech. Both the Obama campaign's decision to reject public financing and the Supreme Court's 2010 *Citizens United* ruling point in this direction. Americans have never been very fond of public financing, at least as judged by the little-used "check off" provision in the federal tax code, and the country seems currently to be moving in the direction of freer political speech.

But efforts continue to find new ways to regulate political speech, and much is at stake in the idea of government regulation of political marketing. Who is to decide how—and on what basis—to regulate the claims of political speech? We have noted the ways in which political campaigns selectively present the idealized images of their candidates. Are we to suppose that government rules would assist voters in thinking for themselves about how this process works? Or that banning negative ads, for example, would make the process of selective image presentation somehow less, and not more, effective?

It seems that here we confront a cure that is worse than the disease. Government regulation would tend inevitably to favor one set of claims, one type of argument, and one linguistic style over others. Since governing is about the broadest claims about how we should live—that is, of justice—what government entity could or should be trusted to regulate these very claims?

Perhaps a less dangerous course than government would be reliance upon the media to establish the basis for what is to count as valid political claims. This, after all, was somewhat the idea behind the mid- to late-twentieth-century notion of an objective "mainstream" mass media. This media would enjoy the power and the standing to establish what is relevant from what is irrelevant, what is valid from what is invalid, the factual from the non-factual, and the normal from what lies outside the "mainstream." But here, too, today's America is currently on a far different course. While portions of the mass media continue to describe their work as mainstream, the grounds for this claim have significantly eroded. Media outlets now contend openly among themselves, each representing its own notion of what is true or important.

It seems, then that the only sensible course is to have faith in the American voter himself. Voters must empower themselves to evaluate the political claims of candidates who are vying for their votes by becoming aware of the vast array of consumer-based marketing strategies utilized to win their votes.

EMPOWERING WISER VOTERS

There are no meaningful protections for voters in American political campaigns. Voters must search out and consider multiple and often conflicting sources of information. They must put hard questions against the claims of political candidates, in order to separate what is true from what is desired. Being a responsible voter requires time, energy, and non-partisan evaluation of the breadth of information that bombards us.

Thus we come full circle to our beginnings as a nation. The necessary condition for responsible voting today is much the same as it has always been. No short cuts are available to determine the truth or falsity of political claims made by candidates. This, after all, is why the First Amendment to the Constitution guarantees free speech to Americans. And this is why that dogged opponent of every form of tyranny over the mind of man, Thomas Jefferson, favored a fully free and independent press without the hint of political or other limitations of any kind. Our leaders are ultimately not the brands which their campaigns have so artfully created; they are people. Voters need to educate themselves to determine who these candidates and leaders truly are.

American voters do not get the government they are promised; they get the government they deserve.[23] Voters must think through the entire political marketing cycle. Voters must be fully aware that the branded candidate is not likely to be the same elected official who will govern once in office.

As voters, we are on our own. An informed and wise citizenry is every bit as—and maybe more—important today than it was in the early days of the republic.[24] There is no institution, or set of institutions, which can substitute for us, the voters. We cannot improve upon the words repeated so often, and in so many contexts, throughout American history: eternal vigilance is the price of liberty. We have to think for ourselves. We each have one voice and one vote. Make it count.

NOTES

This chapter is adapted from Lisa Spiller and Jeff Bergner, *Branding the Candidate: Marketing Strategies to Win Your Vote* (Praeger, 2011), with the permission of the publisher.

1. Ron Chernow, "The Feuding Fathers," *Wall Street Journal*, June 26–27, 2010, W1-2.

2. Hugh Heclo, "Campaigning and Governing: A Conspectus," in *The Permanent Campaign and Its Future*, Norman Ornstein and Thomas Mann, eds. (Washington, DC: American Enterprise Press, 2000), 5.

3. Heclo, "Campaigning and Governing," 5–6.

4. Heclo, "Campaigning and Governing," 6–7.

5. Richard Hofstadter, *The Age of Reform* (New York: Random House, 1955), 257.

6. Kathleen Hall Jamieson, *Packaging the Presidency: A History and Criticism of Presidential Campaign Advertising* (New York: Oxford University Press, 1992), 17.

7. Jamieson, *Packaging the Presidency*, 19–20.

8. Joe McGuiness, *The Selling of the President* (New York: Trident Press, 1969), 192, 195.

9. Roger Kerin, Steven Hartley, and William Rudelius, *Marketing*, 10th ed. (New York: McGraw-Hill/Irwin, 2011), 283.

10. Jay Conrad Levinson, *Guerrilla Creativity: Make Your Message Irresistible with the Power of Memes* (New York: Houghton Mifflin, 2001), 3.

11. Rahaf Harfoush, *Yes We Did: An Inside Look at How Social Media Built the Obama Brand* (Berkeley, CA: New Riders, 2009), 69.

12. Kerin, Hartley, and Rudelius, *Marketing*, 224.

13. Richard J. Semiatin, ed., *Campaigns on the Cutting Edge* (Washington, DC: CQ Press, 2008), 88.

14. David Plouffe, *The Audacity to Win* (New York: Viking/Penguin, 2009), 20.

15. In the 2008 general election, one in ten voters was a first-time voter. This was no different than had been the case in 2004, suggesting that the Obama campaign did not bring as many new voters into the process as has sometimes been said. This was true of the youth vote, for example, which grew only from 47 percent turnout in 2004 to 49 percent in 2008. As previously stated, the Obama campaign excelled in capturing a much larger share of first-time voters, including the youth vote. John Kerry had won first-time voters in 2004 by a margin of 53 percent to 46 percent; Obama's margin over McCain was 69 percent to 30 percent. See Chuck Todd and Sheldon Gawiser, *How Barack Obama Won: A State-by-State Guide to the Historic 2008 Presidential Election* (New York: Random House, 2009), 31.

16. Lisa Spiller and Martin Baier, *Contemporary Direct and Interactive Marketing*, 2nd ed. (Upper Saddle River, NJ: Prentice Hall, 2010), 29.

17. Plouffe, *The Audacity to Win*, 377.

18. John Heilemann and Mark Halperin, *Game Change: Obama and the Clintons, McCain and Palin, and the Race of a Lifetime* (New York: Harper Collins, 2010), 32.

19. Heilemann and Halperin, *Game Change*, 32.
20. Plouffe, *The Audacity to Win*, 261.
21. Harfoush, *Yes We Did*, 116–18.
22. Spiller and Baier, *Contemporary Direct and Interactive Marketing*, 396.
23. Victor Kamber, *Poison Politics: Are Negative Campaigns Destroying Democracy?* (New York: Plenum Press, 1997), 7.
24. John A. Quelch and Katherine C. Jocz, *Greater Good: How Good Marketing Makes for Better Democracy* (Boston: Harvard Business Press, 2007), 197.

III

On the Ends of Liberal Education

SEVEN

Majoring in Servitude

Liberal Arts and the Formation of Citizens

Jonathan Yonan

Not long ago an upper level administrator of a leading regional accrediting body gave an address to the faculty of my university. With the warmth and confidence that attend officials of an ascendant regime, she smiled as she laid out the new realities her organization was implementing. No irony intended, she explained: "We are now entering a brave new world. It's already here. The work ahead for you is catching up with it."

The clear expectation of her words was that the faculty would fall in line with the accreditor's demands. We had to. Why risk losing accreditation when it would mean the loss of federal funding? There was every incentive not to question the principled grounds of the accreditor's authority, their bureaucratic method of oversight, or the value and cost of the impending university-wide process. Besides, for many in higher education such questions about the current academic climate have become needless ivory tower exercises, the stuff of philosophical mumbo jumbo, not the stuff of on-the-ground university administration.

There is no question that universities should be held accountable to standards of excellence, and accreditors may have a role to play. Particularly as academic quality is continually threatened by both rapid grade inflation and the proliferation of ever-more specialized, ever-less meaningful degree programs, what sociologist Randall Collins has called "credential inflation."[1] That said, my concern is the nonchalance with which this official simply assumed that our college faculty would demonstrate that key habit of human servility: willing compliance. A willing, unquestioning compliance, I hasten to add, which stands in stark opposition to that vital habit of any free citizenry: rational discourse.

Rational discourse is necessary for any humane and free society. It is necessary, first, because it enables the freedom of the individual conscience which is most free when it gives assent to those ideas which are justified and likewise rejects those shown to be invalid, no matter how powerful the advocates of the weaker argument are. Second, rational discourse offers a public means of discerning which ideas are good for a polity, which is one of the reasons freedom of expression is so important. Well-reasoned public discourse allows for ideas to be held to a high standard of clarity and coherence, grounded in good reason. Those that fail that standard should be set aside. But in this view freedom of conscience and freedom of expression are not ends in themselves. They are the ethical and political conditions necessary *for* the common good.

To be sure, a free citizenry must be formed with other habits and values besides a commitment to rational discourse. A truly free citizenry must, for example, be formed in the habits of responsibility, otherwise individuals in complacency might believe that it is someone else's duty to tell them what to think and how to live. On the contrary, good citizens will take responsibility to establish their own freedom of conscience by seeking to know what is true and to test those convictions for themselves through rational discourse.

A free citizenry will also require what many have called the moral imagination. Far more important than the modern scientific impulse to explain and measure human excellence by statistical analysis, we must nurture the impulse to marvel at lived examples of such excellence — saints, martyrs, heroes, statesmen — those lives worth emulating. The moral imagination when it is propelled by a sense of responsibility is given the dramatic creativity which tries to embody the sort of human excellence which rational discourse has established as good.

All these things facilitate well-reasoned moral action particularly in the face of some sort of difficulty or opposition. Of course, under threat of consequences it must be said that our university faculty (myself included), like most others, willingly complied with our accreditors' demands. These are the routine bellwethers, I shall argue, of a society which is tipping toward decline — a society which, in turning away from the liberal arts, is increasingly rejecting the core virtues of a free citizenry. This essay explores the rejection of the classical liberal arts tradition by large sectors of our culture and how this rejection is manifesting itself within the Academy. After laying out the classical understanding of the liberal arts, I will discuss the troubling implications of the Academy's movement away from the liberal arts tradition.

The underlying premise about human nature from which liberal arts education derives its value is that we are a species ever inclined toward servility, whether it be servility to the political order, to common opinion, or to our material and economic circumstances. Each generation must make a positive case, therefore, for the liberal arts—for liberty.

For some perspective on this subject, that old conversation between Plato and Aristophanes is worth revisiting. Aristophanes, we should remind ourselves, disagreed with Plato over the moral character of the latter's famous teacher, Socrates. In what is probably his most well-known comedy, *Clouds*, Aristophanes portrays Socrates as a sophist—as a manipulative twister of words, turning any conversation to his own advantage by making the weaker argument the stronger. In fact, in *Clouds*, Socrates goes so far as to peddle his sophistry throughout Athens, training his students in the skills of his rhetorical technique, and teaching them how to weasel out of their civic duties. Of course the comedian's portrait of Socrates could not be in sharper disagreement with Plato's, as depicted in works like *Gorgias* or *Apology*.

Aristophanes and Plato disagreed sharply over Socrates; here is a fascinating conversation worth revisiting. Their conversation dealt directly with a fundamental question with which every human being struggles: *What makes a good life?* It demands an answer from each of us. Every life lived is an answer ventured. Plato's way of framing this question was to ask, *What sort of man was Socrates?*

Aristophanes and Plato present fundamentally inconsistent portrayals of Socrates. In *Clouds* Aristophanes humorously portrays Socrates seeking his own "advantage" in every conversation, manipulating children into rejecting their families and subverting the moral order. This Socrates began conversations by saying: "Tell me a little about yourself. I need to understand your particular personality traits. Then I can correctly determine the best tactics to deploy."[2] This Socrates did not tell the truth. Nor did he seek it. His efforts were spent maneuvering around his interlocutors into rhetorical victory. He sought power.

In contrast to Aristophanes' account, Plato's *Apology* presents Socrates as a philosopher who sought the truth. It is important to note that he was neither an armchair philosopher—aloof with his head in the clouds—nor a professional philosopher—expert specialist in impenetrable theories. Plato's Socrates had no interest in either. For Plato, Socrates is a philosopher because his soul is disposed to or desires what is good and because he loves to pursue it. Socrates is also a philosopher because he has an enlarging soul, by which we mean that the disposition of his soul is, in a sense, contagious. He spreads what is good around through conversation with others. For all of this, Plato's Socrates turns out to be the most human and the most humanizing sort of person.

In his *Apology*—which is Plato's account of the trial in which Socrates is condemned to death—Socrates says, "It is the greatest good for a man to discuss virtue every day . . . for the unexamined life is not worth living."[3] Taken together with his apparently aimless discussions, many have understood this line as a call to the contemplative life—construed as an unending and directionless private intellectual exercise. This is the world of the ideal, but not the real; the good life as the life of ideas *only*, the life of the mind *only*, with no political dimension. The good life would have nothing to do with the active life, with "life in the city," which is the way the Greeks would have put it.

Too often this is our portrait of Socrates. He has his head in the clouds and has no practical use for the city. This, then, is a common misunderstanding of Socrates' life—a series of useless, aimless pie-in-the-sky conversations. Parents of college students put their fingers on this whole business when they ask sharply, *What are you going to do with that major?* Which is another way of saying, *There is such a thing as useless, fruitless study, and it's no good wasting your time on that!* To this point we must observe that for Plato's Socrates the philosopher *is* a political actor, and his business is intensely practical.

This is perhaps best seen in Plato's *Symposium*. The text relates a conversation Socrates had with several of his friends over an entire evening. The subject of their conversation was the nature of *eros*, which Socrates concludes is the immaterial form of Beauty itself, the divine.[4] How much more philosophical could he be? And how impractical!

Not so. As it happens, even as their entire discussion revolves around the impractical subject of divine Beauty, Plato's *Symposium* as a whole is a penetrating assessment of the political soul. The selfish interest of Socrates' conversation partners, it seems, prevents them from seeing and understanding the true nature of *eros*. Therefore, Socrates reasons with them to show how each one has failed to understand; their failure is not due to being overly political, but to the fact that their respective political perspectives impede the pursuit of truth.

Socrates makes his ideas public by saying them. He refuses to tolerate ideas which are false and then he explains why. Socratic discourse is thus inherently political. Simply put, to speak is to be political. To give an argument is to engage in rational politics. In the act of conversation thought itself becomes action; philosophy becomes politics, deploying rational discourse as an assertive, political act. Remember that one gives a reason for an idea because one is trying to assert the idea upon another on the assumption that the reasoned truth of the idea is good grounds to believe it. When we speak we are trying to push our conversation partners in a direction. We even speak of the "force of logic," because reasoned truth has a way of pushing us along its path.

Plato's philosopher does not seek personal victory in rational discourse as sophists do. He seeks to find truth through rational discourse. In a conversation, we ought to reject ideas when they are shown to be false, even if they are our own ideas. Aristophanes' sophistic Socrates, however, does not understand that to be refuted in rational discourse is to be the beneficiary of an act of justice. Indeed, discourse leading to refutation is part and parcel of the best sorts of friendship because it moves friends away from falsehood and toward truth, which is a good thing to desire for those one loves, for one's city, and for oneself. The truth liberates the individual from falsehood, whether that falsehood consists of one's own opinions or the opinions of the city.

This is why sophistry is at once very powerful and very evil. It poses as truthful discourse in order to convince others of its goal, regardless of whether that goal is good or not. It pretends to use valid reason and is successful when it convinces us that its conclusions are based in valid reason even if they are not. Sophistry, then, is dehumanizing because it turns human discourse into a technology of power, a mechanism for getting people to do what the speaker wants them to do. Importantly, where human discourse is the rational engagement between two free persons in pursuit of the truth, the sophist is a cunning imposter who seeks to undermine the rational liberty of his conversation partner.

By most accounts, when this is done to free, rational adults, the condition they enter into is called slavery. The liberal arts tradition of education was specifically developed as a preservative against this very sort of slavery. It was established on the belief, grounded in centuries of human experience, that such slavery is the unchanging tendency of human nature. Current trends in American higher education only seem to reinforce this point.

Consider the arguments made by two leaders of renowned liberal arts institutions in the United States. In a recent interview on CNN, Christopher B. Howard, the president of Hampden-Sydney College—the tenth oldest college in the United States—was asked to defend the value of a liberal arts education in the midst of a tough economy with a high unemployment rate. His answer is revealing. Howard argued:

> You train for what you know, you educate for what you don't know. We don't know what jobs are going to be important in the future. But we know that they are going to be jobs that require critical thinking, practical reasoning, and a good sense of being able to write well, speak well, and good quantitative reasoning skills. A liberal arts education like Hampden-Sydney College, or your Amhersts, your Williams, etc. are going to give you that and that is going to help you going forward.[5]

About a year earlier, Michael Roth, president of Wesleyan University, explained in a somewhat more ennobling fashion that "rather than pursuing business, technical or vocational training, some students (and their families) opt for a well-rounded learning experience [which is] not reducible to the material circumstances of one's life." Roth later added, "the American model of liberal arts education emphasizes freedom and experimentation as tools for students to develop meaningful ways of working after graduation."[6]

Both Howard and Roth agree that what is liberal about the liberal arts is that they liberate us from the unpredictability of the future, which is depicted as the all-menacing time after graduation. For them the liberal arts train people in skills which are always useful in finding economic security in the face of the material uncertainties of the day. That is the sales pitch, at least. The technician's toolbox may have been polished up a bit, but we are still dealing in the training of highly skilled laborers. This is not the liberal arts of the classical Western tradition, though this view of education does try to answer the parent's question, *What are you going to do with a Liberal Arts degree?*

In today's economy it is hard to defend a liberal arts degree because it seems impractical in that it does not pave an automatic path to a job. In response to this challenge and threatened by a crowded undergraduate market—which includes huge state universities, online degree programs, discount community colleges, for-profit universities, and a galaxy of pre-professional certifications—today's messaging is that while an elementary education degree or an accounting degree can certify a student for one job, a liberal arts degree provides a skill set that prepares students for any job now or in the future.

This rhetoric still prioritizes training students for lives of efficiency and productivity—the servile, not the liberal arts. Such marketing feeds on a future-oriented anxiety over job security by promising better tools for dealing with an unknown future. It is the same sales pitch that any pre-professional degree program would use, only grander (and more abstract). Instead of training in practical vocational skills, liberal arts colleges train students in even more practical meta-skills.

Our institutions of higher learning thus produce super-highly skilled practical laborers on the one hand (trained as specialists in research universities and pre-professional programs) and super-highly skilled meta-laborers on the other (trained as generalists in our liberal arts colleges). The training of laborers with a specific skill set, but oriented toward no particular end (other than the content-free "job") is reminiscent of a scenario Mark Twain conjured in his wonderful novel, *A Connecticut Yankee in King Arthur's Court.*

Falling asleep in nineteenth-century New England and waking up in sixth-century England, Hank Morgan manages to think critically and problem-solve his way around the childlike people of Camelot. Within weeks Hank—"a giant among pigmies"[7]—assumes the administrative side of the monarchy. Arthur is King. Hank is the Boss. Within a short space of time as head bureaucrat, Hank steps back to consider the well-oiled machine of a political economy he has created—a new and improved England, complete with an entire educational system producing expert specialists, fine-tuned to the precise requirements of his vision:

> I was pretty well satisfied with what I had already accomplished. In various quiet nooks and corners I had the beginnings of all sorts of industries under way—nuclei of future vast factories, the iron and steel

missionaries of my future civilization. In these were gathered together the brightest young minds I could find, and I kept agents out raking the country for more, all the time. I was training a crowd of ignorant folk into experts—experts in every sort of handiwork and scientific calling.[8]

Hank finally concludes, "My works showed what a despot could do with the resources of a kingdom at his command."[9] In Hank's England, there were no liberal arts. Education was training in the skills necessary to achieve his social vision. He marketed for it. He recruited for it. Then he educated for it. Of course Twain's humorous administrative executive had a progressive vision without much of an imagination. The best he could envisage for sixth-century England was to be reengineered into his own nineteenth-century America.

The desire for control is a desire to use other people to accomplish one's own ends. Often it is simply the meddling desire to tell people how to live their lives. We see this appetite for mastery in Hank Morgan, who knows better than everyone else. He only wants what is best for the English. It just happens that what is best for them is Hank's way of doing things, which is convenient for Hank.

A culture that trains people with skills, that trains people to do what they are supposed to do, is a culture that values slavery and mastery. Alternately, a culture that trains people to engage in rational discourse is a culture that values the liberty of equal persons, friends, even. The problem with liberty is that no one is the master; no one gets to run the show. Rather it is reason itself and the rule of law that have authority. A culture that values liberty above any individual's political aspirations requires presidents to step down at the end of their terms, judges to submit their private agendas to a higher law (the Constitution), and individuals not only to tolerate each other's presence, but to engage in a kind of civic discourse where mere opinion is unsatisfactory compared to carefully reasoned positions.

If there is training proper to liberty (the liberal arts) then there is training proper to slavery as well, only the latter leads to greater power for the trainer, whereas the former places truth and the rule of law over all men as the great good to be desired. Truth humbles everyone and enslaves no one. This is why the sophist, who has no regard for truth, is the enemy of the free society. The sophist, to be frank, seeks mastery. Of course these days no one understands themselves to be educating students for sophistry. Most universities instead claim to educate for *leadership*.

Toward this end, today's undergraduate educators, administrators, and accreditors prioritize four intellectual meta-skills above all others. The meta-skills of today are generally grouped under the rubric of leadership skills. This is a form of leadership which is marketed as an antidote to anxiety over or disdain for a number of perpetual human realities:

uncertainty of the future, the domination of permanent ethical and meta-physical truths, and the problem of knowledge in a world of such sheer scope and size. The new advocates of purportedly liberal education promise their students the power to withstand, to keep up with, and even to set the pace in such a reality. Such promises feed into contemporary disdain and anxieties. To be a leader today, so we are told, one must be trained in the following four meta-skills.

Skill one: data-gathering. Skilled leaders need to know things—to know facts. We live in an information age with indexes, search engines, and databases. We no longer read books to be formed by them, but to get data out of them. With a simple Google Book search we can find the three lines in a book that have the key word we are looking for. Speed-reading courses teach us how to use our eyes and our fingers as technologies of data-gathering. Skilled data gatherers treat ideas as discrete things, as stuff. Here I learn three of them. There I obtain six more. I harvest them. I store them. I save them for later use.

Skill two: deconstruction. Students are to be good theorists, which is to say they are to be skilled at subverting the intentions of a text. Having learned a few critical theories, any nineteen-year-old college student can see after reading just a little of Aristotle's *Politics* that Aristotle is guilty of a specifically Marxist sin, complete with a latent class struggle and an unstated assertion of *bourgeois* power. Or fiddle with the critical theories a bit and Aristotle has invented ethics just to weaken the Nietzschean stronger man over whom he desires to exert his priestly will-to-power. These are just two examples of how early access to the theorists can help students withstand the tyranny of a text—its oppressive religious de-mands, its racism, sexism, capitalism, its homophobia. The ability to de-construct is the ability to the get the better of an idea, to say that an idea is up to something hidden, but something that you can see. It is the ability to burst someone else's balloon, so that they cannot burst yours. It is to make someone else's ideas do what you want them to do.

Skill three: data manipulation. Is there any intellectual skill more high-ly praised, more universally esteemed, more ubiquitously touted on course syllabi than critical thinking? It is the crowning glory of the leader. Already a skillful data-gatherer and deconstructer of ideas, the leader must also be agile, ever-moving himself and his ideas to advance his own purposes. Here the deconstructor becomes something worse: a data-ma-nipulator. The critical thinker is taught to put on the lab coat and take the posture of the scientist looking through a microscope at a universe of ideas and to stand over and above them. The critical thinker is outside systems of thought, unmoored from conventional realities. The critical thinker makes new realities and new systems of thought. Hank Morgan was a fantastic critical thinker.

Skill four: engineering. In the decisive undergraduate years a young person must gain mastery of key rhetorical forms and structures in both essay and speech. Five-paragraph essays, topic sentences, hooks, and thesis statements. Armed with strong communication skills, a student has the ability to package and repackage information, to move an idea in any direction—in the direction of his own choosing. The communicator is something of an engineer. Having collected data, broken it down into usable parts, and having critically sculpted his own reframed worldview, the communicator shapes ideas, engineers them in pursuit of his own given ends so that people will fall in line and do what he wants them to do.

Consider The University of Phoenix, for example, which educates students "to develop the knowledge and skills necessary to achieve their professional goals, improve the productivity of their organizations, and provide leadership and service to their communities."[10] In this passage, extracted from the University's mission statement, there is evidence of both sides of what we can only call the servile arts. The slave (the technician) is given knowledge and skills to improve productivity. The master (the sophist or meta-technician) is given knowledge and skills to provide leadership. In either case, whether you are the boss or you are being bossed around, this is the servile arts. They are two sides of the same coin; the one always implies the other.

In the servile arts of today even character formation can be depicted as a skill. Honesty, for example, becomes a kind of efficiency of relationship and no longer a virtue or value. Such things are productive but not necessarily good unless the good is productivity. Leadership has become the skill of bringing people along, managing them, keeping them on board, moving them toward productivity (rather than the Good)—hence the need for honesty and other core values.

Even individual academic disciplines demonstrate this taste for the servile, and therefore appear to cut against the classical vision of the liberal arts. In some cases, it is because the field itself has been conceived explicitly for training certified technicians: business, accounting, finance, marketing, nursing, engineering, education, communications, social work, physical therapy, even leadership studies. In many cases, such degrees will directly culminate in a state or industry level certification or a series of qualifying examinations in the years immediately following college, clearly indicating that technical proficiency in a specific skill is exactly what is at issue in such programs. Unfortunately, many undergraduate programs in the natural sciences are being recast mainly as technical laboratory training for scientific research, such that the major acts as an effective certification in a productive skill. In all this, we find ourselves on the slave side of the servile arts.

Other disciplines, while of real value, seem increasingly given to the kind of thought which frequently drifts toward sophistry, toward the master side of the servile arts. Consider the social sciences, for example, and how frequently we use them to critically think our way into apparent power over an idea. Linguists explain language. Psychologists demystify the mysteries of our minds. Sociologists explain that we are all guilty of wielding power structures such as gender and race. But, of course, all these points can be subverted, or re-subverted. Linguists cannot escape their own paradigm because it takes language even to think about explaining language. As for psychologists, we might ask them who is qualified to demystify their minds once they've demystified ours? The sociologists may be guilty of the greatest infelicity of mind; having shamed the very structures of class, they seem to have made themselves, the explainers, into the most powerful class of all. In all this, we can all too easily slip toward exerting a sort of sophistical power over others and their ideas.

To be fair, such things are increasingly characteristic of the humanities as well. In many cases such disciplines are not in good heart: philosophy, literature, theology, history, politics, and economics, for example. Many such disciplines have been refashioned, some into so-called sciences (history, politics, and economics), and others into a new kind of theoretical preparation to assess the ideas of the past, deconstruct them, and especially to withstand them. Literature, for example, is no longer principally the cultivation of a full-throated moral imagination, but rather critical theories which are used to judge traditions as tyrannies of classicism, taboos, and superstition.

As the 2008–2009 *Guide to the Core Curriculum* for Harvard University explains, the university's undergraduate core curriculum aims to teach "the critical discernment necessary to understand and assess the route to knowledge within any area." Consider, for example, one such course offering at Harvard:

> Courses in *Literature and Arts A* are designed to provide students with a variety of critical and analytic approaches to literature, and to offer a range of responses to questions such as the following: how does literature function; how are literary genres and traditions constituted and transformed; what are the relations among author, reader, text, and the circumstances in which the text is produced; how is our reading of the literature of the past influenced by the concerns of the present?[11]

Strikingly, literary theory precedes, or even displaces literary appreciation. One learns how to critique, analyze, and respond to our culture's literary legacy before one engages with those texts. With a set of theoretically tinted spectacles one will have a hard time reading a text on its own terms, hearing what it is trying to say. In such circumstances, it is the professor's theoretical slant which will form the way that students critically read texts, not good will toward the author.

So as not to give an unearned pardon to my own discipline, let us consider the field of history in detail—a good discipline that is increasingly bereaved. Many today treat history as politics, which is to say that, for many, history is partisan. It is partisan, they say, both because history is inevitably perspectival (one cannot avoid having a perspective) and because history takes sides, or so *they* say—hence the phrase, "history shows . . ." as in, "history shows the folly of holding to certain class attitudes" or "history shows that the expansion of federal power lasts forever."[12]

From this vantage point history can be reducible to evidence for partisan opinions, which makes this sort of history into a kind of mastery—the slavery of the dead, laboring without consent for the various causes of the living. This is the history of people who are out to win the argument at the cost of the people they purport to study. Such historians will often find themselves endorsing political parties in the classroom, redressing social ills by creating new courses, doing justice to the lost voices of the past by programmatically silencing other voices, and colonizing academic disciplines in order to civilize them.

Others say that history is science. It is the pursuit of *Wissenshaft*—that pristine, finalized scientific knowledge of the past. History as science detects and then applies historical laws and processes. Practitioners of this sort of history see moments like the Battle of the Milvian Bridge and the Investiture Controversy and the passage of the Nineteenth Amendment as molecules or cells in a natural, evolutionary process which advances in a predictable direction or as pulleys and pistons in an historical machine, which runs in an ordered fashion and can be reengineered to produce a better outcome. This sort of history begins to sound like a way of predicting the future. In this way history as science too often becomes history as utility—the dead again serving the ends of the living as they try to anticipate and manipulate the future.

This slave-master dichotomy can be interrupted, however, if historians will recall that persons are to be remembered for their own sakes. Events and movements are about people, not political parties or agendas. Years do not measure quantifiable increments of scientific or utilitarian stuff the way inches do. They are increments of human memory, which is a subset of human consciousness.

If all of this is true, historians ought first to be judged according to their formation in certain virtues and only later by their appropriation of a toolbox of technical skills. The great virtues of the liberally minded historian are, at least, these: charity, decency, and good will to those human neighbors who are no longer able to speak audibly on their own behalf. After all, the remembered past, being human, is not ours to master, for we ourselves find the high-tide of the past gradually filling in all around us. Indeed, we find ourselves all too quickly slipping into the past, and so we have a stake in doing humanist history. Who of us does not desire to be regarded with good will by those who, as yet have not been born?

In 1913, Hilaire Beloc wrote controversially that "the arrangement of society in which so considerable a number of families and individuals are constrained by positive law to labor for the advantage of other families and individuals" is best described as the "servile state."[13]

I would suggest in addition to Beloc's definition that such a state is only possible when certain intellectual preconditions or cultural habits are present, where rational discourse is restrained, where authorities urge, even demand, and where citizens willingly incline toward unquestioning compliance.

Circumstances are rarely so bleak as we may fear. The sky is not falling. Nor do circumstances usually present such prospects for a remedy as we may hope. The liberal arts will not cure our species of our inclination toward servility. To suggest as much and to labor toward such an end would make us no better than Hank Morgan.

Rather, again, we must consider ourselves and our world with all of the disciplinary resources that have always been at our disposal—with rational discourse about the nature of things (philosophy), with the study of the life well lived (ethics), the study of the common good (politics and economics), and the study of how best to speak in defense of the common good (rhetoric), with the moral imagination (literature), with a charitable memory (history), and with the delight and wonder of beholding the natural world of which our very bodies are a part (the natural sciences). These and others are the subjects for consideration in the classical liberal arts tradition, which are to be considered not principally because they contribute to our productivity as a species, nor in an effort to defend ourselves from the tyrannies of tradition, the competitive global market, or the uncertainties of life. Rather, we consider such subjects chiefly because we must understand ourselves and our inclination toward servility, and because we must understand the kind of culture and society which is best suited to human flourishing. In short, we sustain our tradition of liberal learning because we desire not to be slaves to regimes, to individuals, to ideas, or even to ourselves.

The sky is not falling; or perhaps better, the sky is always falling. Liberal learning is the formation of citizens, and only citizens can carry forward the tradition of liberal learning. There is always good work to do in advancing and reclaiming the traditions of liberty and education which are now under our care.

NOTES

1. On grade inflation see, Harvey Mansfield, "Grade Inflation: It's Time to Face the Facts," *Chronicle of Higher Education* 47 (April 2001), B24; Lester H. Hunt, ed., *Grade*

Inflation: Academic Standards in Undergraduate Education (Albany: SUNY Press, 2008); Thomas Bartlett and Paula Wasley, "Just Say 'A': Grade *Inflation* Undergoes Reality Check," *Chronicle of Higher Education* 55 (September 2008), A1–A12. On credential inflation see, Randall Collins, *The Credential Society* (New York: Academic Press, 1979); Randall Collins, "The Dirty Secret of Credential Inflation," *Chronicle of Higher Education* 49 (September 2002), B20; Noel Weyrich, "Failing Grades," *Pennsylvania Gazette* 104 (March/April 2006).

2. Aristophanes, *Clouds*, 478–80.

3. Plato, *Apology*, 38a.

4. Plato, *Symposium*, 211a–212b.

5. See transcript of interview with CNN anchor Ali Velshi, available online at edition.cnn.com/TRANSCRIPTS/1002/23/cnr.06.html (accessed June 15, 2012).

6. "What's a Liberal Arts Education Good For?" *Huffington Post*, December 1, 2008.

7. Twain, *A Connecticut Yankee in King Arthur's Court* (New York: Harper and Brothers, 1917), 66.

8. Twain, *Connecticut Yankee*, 76–77.

9. Twain, *Connecticut Yankee*, 78.

10. See University of Phoenix, "Academic Annual Report 2010," available online at www.phoenix.edu/about_us/publications/academic-annual-report/2010.html (accessed May 28, 2012).

11. See Harvard University, "Introduction to the Core Program," available online at my.harvard.edu/icb/icb.do?keyword=core&pageid=icb.page43827 (accessed June 2, 2012).

12. J. O. Hertzler, "The Sociological Uses of History," *American Journal of Sociology*, 31:2 (September 1925), 187; Mac Johnson, "Bailout: Far Worse than Recession," *Human Events* (September 25, 2008), available online at www.humanevents.com/article.php?id=28716 (accessed November 11, 2011).

13. Hilaire Beloc, *The Servile State* (Indianapolis: Liberty Classics, 1977), 50.

EIGHT

Education to What End—Vocation or Virtue?

Peter A. Benoliel

BACKGROUND: EDUCATION, VOCATION, AND VIRTUE

The above title asks a question about the fundamental purpose of education—*Vocation or Virtue?* Both, I reply, most emphatically!

Before addressing the question directly, a definition of terms is necessary, although utter preciseness is not possible. The term "education" has its root in the Latin *educare*, which means "to lead out." But from what or where does a proper education lead? Instruction and study from the earliest years must enable us to progress from a state of ignorance—or the absence of knowledge—toward the insights that will foster full and productive lives. Education, then, is a process by which one becomes prepared for life and all it entails, including one's individual development and attainment of family, vocation, community, and civic engagement.

The term "vocation" signifies more than just a job or succession of jobs. It includes a multiplicity of activities that enable employment and legitimate sources of income. The word itself has its root in the Latin verb *vocare*—to call—indicating a calling. As Edwin J. Delattre, former president of St. John's College, points out, there is a "difference between a vocation and an occupation, between having a calling and having a job." Having a vocation, according to Delattre, is "characterized as aspiring . . . to a life of fulfillment partly through one's work."[1] So for the purposes of this essay, the term vocation means more than activities that merely enable ready employment and a source of income.

125

Of the three core terms, "virtue" is perhaps the most difficult to define. A dictionary might suggest moral excellence, uprightness and goodness as possible meanings, but even these terms are notoriously difficult to understand. Western philosophers, starting with Plato and Aristotle, have viewed virtue as a vital ingredient of spiritual attainment, social interaction, intellectual enlightenment, citizenship, good government and personal happiness. It is in this broader Aristotelian sense that I use the term "virtue" to encompass the notion of a way of life, a way of behaving that enables a human being to be fulfilled in manifold ways while contributing to the collective good of society.

Though we, for the purposes of this essay, may concede the preliminary definitions above, American society as a whole seems rather confused about the meaning of "education" and its expected outcomes. The vast majority of people look to education as a means to prepare people for work, and here the expectation ends. Hence, a "vocation" or, more to the point, a job, is generally seen as the end goal of education. Some quarrel with that perspective and strongly assert that preparation for gainful employment is merely one part of education's much greater whole. This chapter ventures to demonstrate that education, properly conceived, encompasses more than job training and should be a process that prepares human beings for the fullest possible life and one that guides individuals to develop their greatest potential.

Education should thus nourish the individual's intellectual and spiritual development by teaching students *how* to learn, thereby providing the tools and context they need not only for job training but also to lead meaningful lives. Finally, and most importantly, education is a lifetime pursuit—indeed, it begins with family upbringing—which has the potential of enabling us to transform experience into enlightened wisdom and to prepare us to live productive, satisfying and fulfilling lives, both for ourselves as individuals as well as for the greater community. Such an education prepares us to contribute to the economic vitality of our communities as well as for civic engagement within them.

LEARNING TODAY IN HISTORICAL PERSPECTIVE

We would do well to examine the basic framework of education, beginning with the university system of the Medieval period. The Trivium encompassed grammar, rhetoric and logic, and the Quadrivium included arithmetic, geometry, astronomy and music. The Renaissance ushered in much debate upon the means to effect a proper education. Figures such as Lorenzo Valla, Leonardo Bruni, Phillip Melanchthon and Erasmus discussed the means and purposes of education with particular emphasis on the Trivium—combined with the *Ars Historica*—as the necessary preparation for active participation in the life of the community, the latter in contrast to the Medieval emphasis on preparation for the church.

This brief historical sketch should suggest that a continuing discussion regarding the proper means, ends, and quality of education not surprisingly existed from the very beginning of our nation. In the nineteenth century, Horace Mann sought to expand the reach and impact of education by advocating universal public education. In the twentieth century, John Dewey utilized contemporary psychology to introduce major educational reforms that focused on individualized potential and skill development. Since the late nineteenth century our universities have become more specialized and technical.[2]

Despite these many reforms, America's secondary schools and institutions of higher learning are often providing subpar educational experiences for our students. Naturally, there are exceptions, but here are some disturbing statistics: In 2002, U.S. high school students ranked fourteenth in overall literacy among thirty-four higher-income countries. In computational skills, American high school graduates ranked twenty-fifth among higher-income countries, with a score of 487, just below the Organization for Economic Cooperation and Development's average score of 496.[3] Nor do Americans know much about their own history and form of government. In 2008, 71 percent of Americans failed a basic civic literacy test with an average score of less than 50 percent.[4]

Graduation rates also reveal some appalling trends. In 2011, America's high school graduation rate ranked twenty-first of twenty-eight industrialized nations.[5] Finally, according to a 2010 College Board report, Americans ranked twelfth among industrialized nations in the number of tertiary degrees attained by those between the ages of 25 and 34.[6]

The last several decades have seen numerous reports highlighting the decline of our educational system. The federal government's response, the 2002 No Child Left Behind Act, has enabled some marginal improvements, but these have been accompanied by some unintended, negative consequences. Teaching to pass tests is a far cry from effective educational approaches that foster intellectual curiosity and a sustainable quest for knowledge and wisdom.

Despite the fact that an increasing number of our high school students continue on to higher education, teachers are now reporting that only 63 percent of them seem prepared for college.[7] It is no wonder that just over 50 percent will graduate from college within a six-year period, and a goodly percentage of them will need remedial English in order to pursue their studies.[8] As a result, colleges and universities are forced to do the work that the secondary schools failed to accomplish. The lost time and progress during a prime learning period of a student's life is astounding! Indeed, the need for remedial English and mathematics inhibits institutions of higher learning from attaining what ought to be their true goal—enabling students to reach their highest potential.

In 1799, Thomas Jefferson wrote that doing mathematical computations was a "delicious luxury."[9] This is clearly no longer the case. Without a sufficiently sound foundation in mathematics and science, children in the United States will not be prepared for higher education and the training they will need in a technological and knowledge-intensive economy. In turn, the U.S. workforce will not be competitive in the global marketplace.

A recent profile of college graduates indicates that slightly over 1.6 million bachelor's degrees were conferred by all institutions of higher education. The majority of these degrees (52 percent) were in very specific vocational fields, while the remaining degrees included such disciplines as liberal studies, mathematics, philosophy, religion, the life and physical sciences, engineering, psychology and the social sciences.[10] At best, then, just under half of our students have the *possibility* of attaining something that *may* more broadly prepare them for both life and a vocation. I do not wish to imply that the remaining half of our students are ill-prepared. Rather, I merely suggest that roughly half of our students have pursued and received a rather narrow educational/training experience that informs only a portion of a human's most fundamental desires and concerns. Not only will these graduates be less likely to explore the meaning of a full and productive human life, but their attained skills are likely time bound because the "knowledge" they have acquired may be obsolete in a few years and, most likely, will have confined their options, skill sets, expectations and outlook.

Of the 52 percent receiving degrees in specific vocational pursuits, some 348,000 students (or about 21 percent) received degrees in business and management.[11] Their undergraduate years could have been better spent in pursuing the liberal arts, including in-depth exposure to the humanities and rigorous instruction in the physical, life and social sciences. I can categorically state, having enjoyed a business career of forty years at the highest levels, that an undergraduate degree in business administration *at best* prepares an individual for entry-level positions. Such degrees in no way prepare a student for advancement and leadership. To be sure, a business degree may open the door to an entry-level job, but that is often the extent of it. Much of what a business degree encompasses is theoretical and in many cases obsolete; it will hardly cultivate the intellectual and spiritual development that is prerequisite for business leadership or meaningful civic engagement.

THE BENEFITS OF LIBERAL EDUCATION IN
THE REAL BUSINESS WORLD

Perhaps my own observations regarding business and organizational leadership, gleaned from my experience as the chief executive officer

(CEO) of a global company for twenty-five years, as well as having served on a number of corporate boards and chaired more than a handful of cultural and civic organizations, might provide some useful insights as to the genuine worth of the liberal arts. My formal educational experiences were at a highly regarded university where I majored in philosophy, with minors in music and chemistry, followed by three years in the U.S. Navy, where I was trained as a line officer with a "specialty" in marine engineering. I acquired, through self-study and experience, technical, scientific, financial, legal, marketing, manufacturing, and leadership skills.

But how did my liberal education, ongoing as it continues to be, prepare me for business leadership? It helped me develop and hone my problem-solving and analytical skills; my ability to synthesize—that is, to maintain a balanced consideration of factors; my critical judgment; and my leadership and interpersonal skills, through engaging and conversing with some of the best teachers history has to offer—to name a few, Homer, Plato, Thucydides, Aurelius, Shakespeare (Henry V on the eve of battle), and Abraham Lincoln.

Two examples from my own career demonstrate the fruits of ongoing liberal learning. The first relates to the time (1966) when I became the CEO of Quaker Chemical Corporation and assembled my top management team for our first meeting. I posed the question, "What are we in business for?" There was nervous laughter and rolling of eyes as the answer seemed obvious—"to make a profit." After a number of remarks along this line, a long silence followed. It took two meetings—over six hours—for us to arrive at the following answer: "To achieve and maintain a profitable rate of operation (the means) and thus to enhance the lives of our stakeholders (the ends)." We next asked, "Who are our stakeholders?" These were identified as our shareholders, employees, customers, suppliers, and the communities in which we conduct our operations. Some years later, we broadened the list to include the environment. While today such corporate creeds are not uncommon, a half century ago the development of such a creed proved to be both challenging and novel.

The corporate scandals of the last twenty-five years and the more recent 2007–2008 banking/economic collapse, which were brought about in large measure by practices on Wall Street and parts of the business community, indicate that businesses and corporations have narrowed their perspectives and are therefore losing sight of their responsibility to their larger community of stakeholders. Today's corporations tend to focus on the short-term, which entails the maximization of profits and what's best for top executives rather than longer-term and broader concerns for all who have a stake in an organization's well-being and sustainability. We correctly understood our company's sustainable success as inextricably linked to the well-being and enrichment of all the people who were the stakeholders of the enterprise. In contrast to the outsized compensation of top management today, we looked to achieve internal proportionality among our employees, from factory hands to the CEO. After all, we were creating a team and a sense of shared success and reward.

We understood that the task of management was to balance the rewards to the stakeholders while acknowledging the inherent conflict among them. To maximize returns to shareholders is to slight the legitimate expectations of employees or customers or the community at large. While seeking a balance, we were endeavoring to achieve long-term sustainability and hopefully meeting the reasonable expectations of our stake-holders.

The strongly held and practiced values that enabled us to run our business so successfully had their roots in the liberally educated individuals who were collectively making the decisions. These people had developed their values and outlooks from lessons learned from literary and religious texts, philosophical treatises, and the arts, as well as life experience. The lessons of the liberal arts endure, as does the Quaker Chemical enterprise some forty-five years later.

A second aspect of my experience illustrates the value of both formal and ongoing liberal learning. A proper understanding of one's place in the world and one's relationship with fellow human beings—be they family, organizational associates, customers, or the "other party" in negotiations—is paramount in the conduct of business. Indeed, success in organizational leadership and negotiation is squarely dependent upon one's understanding and appreciation of "the other guy"—knowing his values, needs, and objectives, and treating him fairly and appropriately. All this is easily said but difficult to practice consistently. Educational background is essential to becoming an effective practitioner. One would do well to study leaders of the past—both real and the fictional—the Bible, the Greek playwrights, Thucydides, Plutarch, Shakespeare (always Shakespeare!), Jane Austen, George Eliot, Joseph Conrad, and the biographies of such leaders as Lincoln, Mahatma Gandhi, Martin Luther King Jr., and Nelson Mandela, to see how they were challenged by and mastered these important lessons.

Success in my most difficult negotiations and situations hinged on my ability to put myself on the other side of the table so I could, as best as possible, understand the values, the material/financial goals, and the emotional needs of my negotiating partners. Abraham Lincoln was a genius in this regard.

AMERICA'S CHANGING ECONOMIC LANDSCAPE

In order to understand the skills needed in today's business environment—and to further defend the liberal arts as preparatory for such a vocation as well as for life—consider the impact that automation is having on today's workplace. Computers and related information technologies have enabled the acceleration and multiplicity of the processes of production, financial transactions, and information sharing. In turn, this has translated into the loss of millions of jobs.[12] Indeed, computer technology has brought about major discontinuities in our economy and society that only can be compared to the Industrial Revolution.

Our educational institutions must respond to the changing nature of the workplace and the concomitant skills required.[13]

From Hands-on to Hands-off: Skills in the emerging economy are increasingly peripheral to hands-on work. As technology subsumes the repetitive aspects of work, human labor becomes peripheral to the actual fabrication of goods and delivery of services.

From Particular to General: As the context for using skills shifts from repetitive applications to varied uses, skills requirements are shifting from the job-specific to more general competencies.

From Concrete to Abstract: Increasingly, jobs require that workers spend more time sitting in front of computer screens wrestling with abstractions. As physical tasks become mental tasks and thinking becomes procedural, communication and higher-order conceptual skills become more important for making the abstract more concrete.

From Repetition to Handling Exceptions: Because of the reach of technology into work functions, human capital is used more and more to handle exceptions to routine production and service delivery. Continuous processes and shared information are replacing sequential work processes.

From Solitary to Interactive: In the new economy, jobs require interacting with colleagues, suppliers and customers. Hierarchies are in decline, and informal networks are more important.

Narrow vocational training is hardly suited to prepare a workforce for successful engagement with the new economy. Supervisory and non-supervisory workers today need a reservoir of skills that are deeper and broader than heretofore required on the job. This means that people who aspire to obtain and hold jobs in the new workplace must have a broad array of skills that enable them to learn in a rapidly changing technological environment, to deal with and conceptualize the abstract, to undertake complex problem-solving, and to interact effectively in a non-hierarchical structure. We should consider whether the average high school graduate or vocationally trained college graduate will "cut the mustard."

Given the comparatively low rates of literacy, borderline comprehension skills, and weak computational abilities that characterize today's high school graduates, it would hardly seem so. Not only is their employability marginal, at best, but these deficiencies may very well put our country's economic well-being at risk. Indeed, despite high unemployment rates among recent high school and college graduates, several million unfilled job openings now exist, a depressingly stark indication of this problem.

TODAY'S EDUCATIONAL CHALLENGE

Of course, all of this concern for skill sets and appropriate workplace preparation barely addresses the greater goals of education—that is, the concern for fostering human potential, individual growth, and responsible citizenship.

Many initiatives, particularly No Child Left Behind and Race to the Top—with all of their shortcomings—attempt to address the dire results of primary education in America. The proliferation of charter and private schools as options to the public school system may provide hopeful signs of the American people's economic and political will to create better outcomes for their children and for society.

No Child Left Behind intended to raise national standards of proficiency, but led to unfortunate priorities in the classroom. I contend that national standards be kept in place but that they must be modified to ameliorate present practices. Standards ought to include minimum proficiency in a second language; understanding of the scientific method and principles in both the life and physical sciences; and civic literacy, including rudimentary knowledge of our governmental institutions, their history, and their functions.

A further word in regard to civic literacy is in order. A survey by the National Constitution Center revealed that 41 percent of respondents were not aware there were three branches of government, 62 percent could not name them, and 33 percent could not even name one. Based on these statistics, journalist Eric Lane writes,

> The goal of civic literacy is to continuously reinvigorate our democracy through the promotion of meaningful civic engagement. It requires knowledge of the Constitution, its history, and its values, as they have evolved. We have to understand the fragility of our democracy and our obligation to maintain it. The only place to start is with the public schools.

Lane cites Michael Sandel's observation that without civic literacy "there is no continuity between present and past, and therefore, no responsibility, and therefore, no possibility for acting together to govern ourselves."[14] Citizens will more likely focus on immediate concerns and fail to gain the insight or foresight to solve America's future challenges. Only through civic education in our schools (K–12) will we be able to ameliorate this condition.

While difficult to measure and probably not susceptible to national standards, we should insist that no one graduate from high school without a grounding in our country's rich cultural, religious and historical heritages. We owe this to all our youth whether they have higher educational ambitions or not. We must also adequately prepare them for employment in the new workplace, hopefully enabling them to know how to learn, thus providing the basis of greater self-awareness and self-development as they mature. It is only in this way that our nation can hope to have a viable economy and responsible government. In sum, this would be a preparation for work, citizenship and life.

Universal national service, without exemption, for all young Americans—male and female, physically and mentally challenged, between the ages of seventeen and thirty—would go a long way to compensate for the present and future deficiencies in our nation's secondary schooling.[15] Options could include military service, the Peace Corps, or conservation corps, among others. Pay scales and ranks would be identical across the services. No one could be discharged without having attained established levels of standards in reading, writing, comprehension, mathematics, computer skills, and problem-solving.

The military and other national services have a proven record of success in their training activities and outcomes, to which I can personally attest from my Naval experience. The benefits of two years of national service are manifold. First, such service would connect all citizens to the body national—inculcating the democratic principles upon which this nation was founded. Second, it would produce a more highly and broadly prepared workforce to satisfy the requirements of the changing workplace in a global economy. Finally, it would engender a collective civic consciousness which would lead to increased civic engagement.

The federal expenditures needed to support such a program would be an investment that would yield extremely high rates of return (far greater than most other government expenditures or outlays) while accomplishing high-priority national objectives. Such service would provide America's youth with the proper training for work and for life. Put another way, it would be an investment in human capital, America's most precious asset.

DUTIES OF COLLEGES AND UNIVERSITIES

In conclusion, let's consider what ought to be the substance of higher education in America. In addition to schools (K-12) ensuring basic reading, writing, mathematical and computer skills, colleges and universities must ensure adequate levels of scientific reasoning and world historical knowledge. In so doing, they must prepare students to cope with a rapidly changing technological and global environment, thus the context for vocational training in manifold fields. And, most importantly, nourish the minds, the hearts, and the spirits of our young people, thus preparing them for civic engagement.

Such goals require that we return to our nation's touchstone, the Declaration of Independence. Amid the bewildering and oftentimes unseemly antagonisms of special and narrow interests, U.S. citizens generally share Thomas Jefferson's vision of "life, liberty and the pursuit of happiness" as rights to which all citizens are entitled. Indeed, despite our nation's conflicts over the central purpose of education, Jefferson's immortal words can provide a basis of shared aspirations for America's educational systems. These famous words reflect Jefferson's educational background, schooled as he was in Greek and Roman history and philosophy, as well as his immersion in the zeitgeist of the Age of Enlightenment, where happiness was considered a "birthright . . . coincident with virtue."[16] Perhaps these notions ought to inform America's educational system.

Life: Our educational offerings ought to open doors to the breadth and depth of human knowledge, expand horizons, develop intellectual faculties, challenge individual opinions, and nourish spirits. That is, it ought to prepare us to live life to the fullest, both as individuals and as part of our communities. Such a preparation for life would entail preparedness for a vocation. Shirley Tilghman, president of Princeton University, similarly suggests that "liberal education is designed to prepare you not for *one* profession but for *any* profession, including those not yet invented."[17]

Liberty: Students need to be well versed in the liberal arts, just as were our forefathers who framed the Constitution. The Latin root *artes liberalis*, after all, literally means "the arts of a free man." An ability to read and gain insight from Homer, Thucydides, Plato, Aristotle, Cicero, and Locke enabled the Founders to devise the values upon which this nation was built. Their education also shaped their courage that enabled them to risk their lives, their fortunes and their sacred honor to overthrow what they deemed to be the despotic rule of Great Britain. They understood that freedom, to be maintained, carried with it concomitant responsibilities and obligations. As James Madison succinctly explained, "A well-instructed people alone can be a permanently free people."[18]

The U.S. Constitution fairly demands the understanding and participation of an informed citizenry and active civic engagement. Our liberty and our lives as a free people can only be guaranteed through enlightened participation. Our forefathers, educated as they were—certainly skilled in the Trivium (grammar, rhetoric, logic)—had every expectation that the future citizens of the United States would be similarly educated and prepared for civil responsibility. How else would they be able to sustain, in Abraham Lincoln's words, "government of the people, by the people, for the people"?[19]

Pursuit of Happiness: The final and perhaps most difficult notion posed by Thomas Jefferson is "the pursuit of happiness." Jefferson derived this phrase from John Locke's "life, liberty and property" in Locke's *Second Treatise of Government*. Jefferson intentionally and monumentally altered Locke's phrase from "property" to the ambiguous "the pursuit of happiness." The right to own property is something most Americans hold near and dear to their hearts—it is a concrete idea guaranteed by several clauses of the Constitution. But the notion of "the pursuit of happiness" begs definition. To venture a definition, we must consider some of the other important figures who influenced Jefferson's thinking.

Jefferson was well acquainted with the ancient Greek philosophers. Socrates was the first to begin to ask such revolutionary questions as "What is virtue?" and "What constitutes the good life?" His pupil and disciple, Plato, captured these questions and hints of answers in such compelling dialogues as the *Crito, Meno,* and *Protagoras*. And finally, Plato's pupil, Aristotle, offered more precise descriptions of happiness, the good life and, indeed, virtue.

We can be virtually certain that Jefferson had read the *Nicomachean Ethics* in which Aristotle discusses at length what constitutes happiness for a man. Oversimplified, it goes something like this: a man achieves virtue and, in turn, happiness by developing and practicing good habits of conduct—not engaging in excesses or deficiencies but practicing the "Golden Mean" in his behavior—and by being a contributing member of society and recognized as such. A man's happiness is wrapped up in something beyond himself—a higher purpose than himself—namely, living as a contributing member of society and in harmony with that society. A man who is able to do so throughout his life indeed achieves virtue and happiness, intertwined as they are. Jefferson had in mind this broad definition of happiness in crafting the words of the Declaration of Independence. Should not our educational system enable students to lead lives pursuing such an exalted conception of virtue and happiness?

WHY BOTH VOCATION AND VIRTUE?

The inadequacies of America's secondary and higher educational systems are well documented. The unfortunate result is that a majority of our young people are destined to uncertain economic futures, unable to find jobs that characterize the present global/digital age. In turn, the competitive global position of the United States is very much in jeopardy. As importantly, our high school graduates, not to mention our drop-outs, are unable to obtain gainful employment, participate in civic life, and realize their own personal intellectual and spiritual potential. Universal national service should be put in place to enable proficiency in the skill sets required by today's economy, as well as educational curricula with outcomes that meet national standards and that include familiarity with our historical and cultural heritage, set in the context of other (Middle Eastern, African and Asian) cultural traditions.

Each and every young person in this country deserves this minimum, both through our schools and national service. It sounds like a tall order, but our nation and many schools have done it in the past, and some are doing it today. It is a question of societal expectations and political will. We owe nothing less to our children if they are to be prepared for the workplace, to be thoughtful, engaged citizens and to lead productive, fulfilling lives. Such a broadly encompassing education as I recommend, both for our high school and college students, is the best preparation for gainful employment, engaged citizenship, responsible leadership, and a virtuous life.

Taken together, vocation, citizenship and virtue encompass what is meaningful, satisfying and, perhaps, noble in life. Our system of education, both secondary and higher, should enable and nourish the greatest within us. Robert Goheen, former president of Princeton University and ambassador to India, put it most eloquently when he stated that an education at its best has the power "to nourish a mind" and "enliven and enlarge a man's conscious jurisdiction to draw out our potential for awareness for rational understanding. It seems to extend our capacities for beneficial service, for responsible action, wherever we happen to find our chosen work."[20]

NOTES

1. Edwin J. Delattre, "Real Career Education Comes from the Liberal Arts," *Teaching Political Science* 10 (1983): 116–18.

2. Meanwhile, such figures as Alec Meiklejohn, Robert Hutchins, Stringfellow Barr, Scott Buchanan and Mortimer Adler have been earnest and effective proponents of the liberal arts as the core of higher educational endeavors.

3. Organization for Economic Cooperation and Development (OECD), *PISA 2009 at a Glance* (OECD Publishing, 2010), 7–9, 17–18, available online at dx.doi.org/10.1787/9789264095298-en (accessed June 15, 2012).

4. Intercollegiate Studies Institute, "The Shaping of the American Mind," available online at www.americancivicliteracy.org/2010/summary_summary.html (accessed June 15, 2012).

5. OECD (2011), *Education at a Glance 2011: OECD Indicators* (OECD Publishing, 2011), 44, available online at dx.doi.org/10.1787/eag-2011-en, 44 (accessed June 15, 2012).

6. John Michael Lee, Jr., Kelcey Edwards, Roxanna Menson, and Anita Rawls, *The College Completion Agenda 2011 Progress Report*, College Board Advocacy and Policy Center, available online at completionagenda.collegeboard.org/sites/default/files/reports_pdf/Progress_Report_2011.pdf (accessed June 15, 2012).

7. National Center for Education Statistics, nces.ed.gov/fastfacts/display.asp?id=372 ; Jason Koebler, "High Schoolers Say Education Necessary to Get Jobs," *U.S. News,*

March 9, 2011, available online at www.usnews.com/education/high-schools/articles/ 2011/03/09/high-schoolers-say-college-education-necessary-to-get-jobs (accessed June 5, 2012).

8.   U.S. Department of Education, National Center for Education Statistics, *The Condition of Education 2011* (NCES 2011-033).

9.   Thomas Jefferson to William Green Munford, June 18, 1799, in Jean M. Yarbrough, *The Essential Thomas Jefferson* (Indianapolis: Hackett, 2006), 193.

10.   U.S. Department of Education, National Center for Education Statistics, Higher Education General Information Survey (HEGIS), "Degrees and Other Formal Awards Conferred" surveys, 1970–71 through 1985–86; and 1990–91 through 2008–09 Integrated Postsecondary Education Data System, "Completions Survey" (IPEDS-C:91–99), and Fall 2000 through Fall 2009.

11.   U.S. Department of Education, National Center for Education Statistics, 1998–99, 2003–04, and 2008–09 Integrated Postsecondary Education Data System, "Completions Survey" (IPEDS-C: 98–99), and Fall 2004 and Fall 2009.

12.   It must be noted that the transplantation of jobs overseas has been a large factor as well.

13.   I have synthesized text from several sources, but principally from a policy statement entitled *American Workers and Economic Change* by the Committee for Economic Development (CED) 1995.

14.   Eric Lane, "America 101," *Democracy: A Journal of Ideas* 10 (Fall 2008): 53–63.

15.   Under my proposal, there would be no exemptions, with possible exceptions for cases of severe mental or physical disability. There would also be deferment for continuing education, but the service requirement would continue to be two years.

16.   Alan Charles Kors, "Why '*The Pursuit of Happiness*'?" unpublished essay in the possession of the author.

17.   Shirley M. Tilghman, speech at The Lawrenceville School, April 6, 2010.

18.   James Madison, "Second Annual Message," December 5, 1810, in Gaillard Hunt, ed., *The Writings of James Madison*, 9 vols. (New York: G. P. Putnam's Sons, 1900–1910), 8:127.

19.   Abraham Lincoln, "Gettysburg Address," November 19, 1863, in Roy P. Basler et al., eds., *The Collected Works of Abraham Lincoln*, 9 vols. (New Brunswick, NJ: Rutgers University Press, 1953–1955), 7:17–23.

20.   Robert Goheen, "Why Teachers—Scholars?" unpublished speech delivered in Chicago and New York City, April 1960.

NINE

"Reflection and Choice"

The Problem and the Promise of the Liberal Arts in America

John Agresto

When it came to liberal education, America's Founding generation had something of the same mixed views that we have. They, as we, were of two minds about the value of the liberal as opposed to the more useful and productive arts. On the one hand, by the time we established ourselves as a nation, we had colleges of learning in almost every state. These were generally founded as religious institutions, to be sure, but each was devoted to improving the life of the mind as well as the salvation of souls. Nor can anyone today look at the lives of Jefferson or Adams or Madison or indeed so many of the great Founders of this nation and not be impressed by the sweep and depth of their learning. We today cannot even read a page of *The Federalist Papers* without being struck by the breadth of classical and historical knowledge not only of the Founders themselves but also of those who were reading what they were writing in the newspapers of the day.

On the other hand, we knew we were an agricultural and commercial people, a nation of progress and production, and in any contest between the liberal and the productive arts, the liberal arts were very often found on the short end. In his first Thanksgiving proclamation, for example, Washington noted the acquisition and diffusion of useful knowledge as a particularly worthy blessing of the Almighty. No mention was made in the proclamation of any particular gifts of liberal learning. In this he was echoing something of the words of the Constitution itself, which singles out the importance of "Science and useful Arts," as entitled to particular national protection.[1]

Even Jefferson—no slouch he when it came to being liberally educated—as the time came to establish various schools at the University of Virginia, urged that a college be set up that would offer instruction to such artisans as "machinists, metallurgists, distillers, [and] soapmakers. . . ." These various useful, mechanical, and manual trades would, by Jefferson, have their studies graced with the title "philosophy." To be exact, they would be called colleges of "technical philosophy." Remember, moreover, the American Philosophical Society, which Benjamin Franklin founded in 1769, was a society established specifically for the promotion of "useful Knowledge," that is, for the promotion of science understood as the mastery of nature and improvement of the human condition and not simply its comprehension. Thus, Franklin would write for the society essays on such "philosophical" matters as the cause and cure of smoky chimneys and on stoves that could consume all their own gasses. Worthy topics without doubt, but hardly what we today would recognize as "liberal."[2]

A century earlier, the same themes of usefulness and productivity were already at work. In 1691, Sir Edward Seymour, Commissioner of the Royal Treasury, rebuffed the Rev. Dr. James Blair, founder and first president of the College of William and Mary, who had gone to England to see if he could raise funds to start a university. When he said that he needed money so that a college could be started that might train young men for the ministry and thus help save souls in the New World, Seymour bellowed, "Souls? Damn your souls! Grow tobacco!"[3] No doubt Blair would have gotten much the same response if he had said his college had hoped to improve men's intellect as well as save their souls.

Examples could be multiplied, all carrying the same theme—Americans are historically ambivalent in our estimation of liberal education. We may not fully understand it, but we seem to respect it, and we think it must be something important, worthy of great minds, rarefied, highly scholarly and intellectual. But Americans also praise the useful arts and generally reward the inventor and doer far more than the thinker. Up to a point, we admire the intellectual, though we do often snicker at his bumbling and tell jokes about his absentmindedness and even his blindness to the real world. We rarely make fun of the artisan in the same way, and we admire what he knows, appreciating that we profit greatly from his expertise. We tend to respect liberal education from a distance while always unsure of what good it produces; yet we know what good other forms of education produce, and we support them and encourage their thriving.

Not long after the work of the Founding generation was complete, Alexis de Tocqueville noted that everything which is particularly American—our religious beliefs, our habits, our commercial nature, everything—seems to conspire "to divert [our] minds from the pursuit of science, literature and the arts . . . and to fix the mind of the American upon purely practical objects. His passions, his wants, his education, and everything about him seem to unite in drawing the native of the United States earthward." To be certain, literacy is universal in society, and so the life of the mind is opened to all. But we soon learn that "the labors of the mind," can be turned from learning for its own sake toward practicality, and that learning can be "a powerful means of acquiring fame, power, or wealth."

In America, Tocqueville noticed, "everyone is in motion, some in quest of power, others of gain. In the midst of this universal tumult, this incessant conflict of jarring interests, this continual striving of men after fortune, where is that calm to be found which is necessary for the deeper combinations of the intellect." To us, "every machine that spares labor, every instrument that diminishes the cost of production, every discovery that facilitates pleasures or augments them, seems to be the grandest effort of the human intellect." In brief, unlike science and the arts in more aristocratic societies, Americans "will habitually prefer the useful to the beautiful, and they will require that the beautiful should be useful."[4]

We may wish we were not so practical and utilitarian, but that is the kind of citizen American democracy produces. We do not, generally, despise the scholar or the theorist or the professor of poetry or the student of ancient and dead languages, but neither do we find any of them all that helpful. We do prefer the useful to the merely theoretical and academic; and we do want even the beautiful to be useful.

Consider, for example, the following comparison between Abraham Lincoln and Edward Everett, both of whom gave speeches at Gettysburg in 1863. Lincoln, unlike Jefferson or Madison, was a man unschooled in the study of the liberal arts. Though "unschooled," Lincoln was by any measure liberally educated in ways that those who teach the liberal arts today can only view with astonishment. Lincoln had, by his own admission, about a year of schooling "all-totaled." He rarely read any of the classical philosophers, nor Sophocles or Aeschylus or Euripides, and little classical history. He never, it seems, read a word of Locke or Hobbes. Instead, he read Jefferson and Shakespeare, and studied the Bible and Euclid.[5] He studied to sharpen his mind, to find insight to his country's most pressing issues, and to discover for himself models of what a man's life should be like. In other words, though unschooled, he knew exactly what the liberal arts could contribute to both a private life and to a nation.[6]

Edward Everett, by contrast, was an editor, Harvard scholar and professor, congressman, ambassador, and governor—one of the most liberally educated and famous orators of his day. Everett gave the careful, elegant, and learned speech at Gettysburg on the same platform with Lincoln. Everett spoke for two hours in a way only the academy can pro-

duce: a speech laden with classical allusions, literary references, mytho-
logical figures, and long, elegant, and ornate phrasing. Lincoln's address
was only fifteen lines. Yet today, the only reason any of us remember
Professor Everett, if ever we do, is that he stood where Lincoln, the unschooled man, spoke, at a ceremony in a graveyard in Pennsylvania.[7]

If anything, our view today of the academic life seems even more
bifurcated than it was in Tocqueville's time or Lincoln's. On some days, it
seems, we toss out whole sectors of learning as mere bookishness and
pedantry or, worse, the rubbish of dead white males. But sometimes we
are sure (regardless of the evidence) that exposure to the humanities will
make us finer people and better citizens of the world; perhaps make us
more humane, even more human. We have the same chaotic view of our
teachers. Sometimes we proclaim that all intellectuals are, as a class, truncated creatures, people who think that book-learning is a substitute for
life, people living in the cloud-cuckoo-land of irrelevant theories and
ideas disconnected from the work and workings of the real world. But
later on we trot out the professor of literature or sociology or philosophy
to help us with every problem, real or imagined. Today humanists and
social scientists are on every talk show, ever so ready to teach us about
race relations or to show us how all wars stem from America's excessive
consumption and disregard of the natural environment, or show us how
to improve the economy while solving the problem of investor greed. So,
not really knowing what the liberal arts are or can offer, we wind up both
disdaining and exalting them in turn.

Despite these latent sentiments of veneration for the liberal arts, many
still question their worth and connection to the real world. Americans
often have difficulty seeing liberal education's relationship to the useful,
the practical, and to the world of work. The liberal arts and liberal education itself began in the instruction of aristocratic men, free men, men who
had leisure and who did not have to worry about working. Others, not of
their class, might have to acquire more work-a-day skills—others would
have to learn how to be soldiers or farmers or artisans of one kind or
another—but freemen need not learn a trade or learn how to be of service
to others. They could enjoy learning not "for use" but "for its own sake."
Over the centuries, we have turned and expanded the words: we have
gone from speaking of a liberal education as simply the education of
freemen, that is, the education of gentlemen, to something more like an
education pursued in leisure that is *fit* for freemen and free women, an
education which leads us to be thinkers and knowers more than workers
or producers. We have expanded the character of the students of the
liberal arts from non-working and aristocratic males to all men and wom-
en who want to see the world more widely and understand life more
generally. But "liberal education" still has at its core the old notion of
learning for the sake of knowing and not learning for the sake of use.
Studying poetry or mathematics is "liberal"; it means to furnish the

minds of thoughtful students with insight and ideas and connections. A nursing program, however, is not called liberal because it is connected to work; it is meant to produce good nurses.

But America is not a land of aristocratic leisure. Despite the fact that we have invented a whole array of tools and implements to do the work of animals and humans, we are not, as a people, leisured as the nobility of old. We all work. We have, to be sure, "free time," and we use that time to refresh ourselves or entertain ourselves; but, still, we are not a people of leisure. Yes, we do carve out a time for our children to have leisure—four years, sometimes more, to avoid the shop or the plow and go to university, to study and not to work: four years (if one goes to a good liberal arts institution) to study art and history and languages. But, after that, whether one studied the liberal arts or studied for a career, one begins to work. How odd might it seem to the citizens of antiquity that the freest people ever in all history devote their lives to work. But we do.

Given the American obsession with work and career goals, it is strange that Americans spend enormous sums to build universities to educate young people in subjects that have no obvious connection to their careers. Why do we often encourage the best of our students to spend at least four years in studies that have no bearing on how they will spend the rest of their working lives? In Europe, indeed in almost all the rest of the world, going to university rarely means studying the liberal arts but studying instead the basics of one's coming trade or occupation. It would seem, paradoxically, that only in America, the land of work itself, are our finest men and women given a respite from all considerations of work.

Ironically, most students do not take advantage of this offering. Most begin their careers in college by studying what is most basic and needful for their future jobs. But still we take what are arguably the best of our students and invite them, nay encourage them, to spend time learning science and literature and history, subjects that they will never "put to use." How do we justify this?

One common justification is to reassure everyone—citizens, parents, the students themselves—that the liberal arts are not disconnected from work at all! Indeed, at their best, they are a kind of "pre-work," a preparation for all sorts of professions or careers. We say, for example, that our graduates of liberal arts universities have studied so much in so many diverse areas, learned so much from their books, that they can, upon graduation, do pretty much anything they choose. We sometimes go so far as to say that the liberal arts are not simply the best preparation for a career, but for all careers. Yet, even as we say this, we know it is not fully or even perhaps mostly true. Most careers need training in the customs, needs, and techniques of the field. Just because one knows plenty about, say, Moliere or Old Norse grammar, does not mean he or she will do well in the financial markets or the airlines industry.

Perhaps a more refined argument would be that the habits, skills, and qualities of mind and imagination fostered in an undergraduate liberal arts environment—habits such as listening sympathetically, arguing and presenting carefully, reading closely—will help students succeed in almost any field they ultimately choose. Still, it seems strange to claim that the liberal arts perfect these skills better than other forms of education. Does not a professional education teach care in reading, listening, and speaking? Might not vocational training, where the consequences of inattention can be far worse, perhaps even deadly, assiduously teach many of these skills as well?

The argument that defends the liberal arts as the nursery of future success says a very odd thing—that the education in what will soon be central to our students' lives comes *after* their liberal arts education: that it is the illiberal instruction of graduate school or the learning that comes with dedication to the job itself that actually does that educating for which the liberal arts were merely preparatory. Contrary to all our occasional talk about the joy and value of liberal learning "for its own sake," very often the best that those who guide our colleges and universities can say of the liberal arts is that they are "preparatory"—that if they are not themselves professional they are surely "pre-professional." What else can we mean when we say that the value of liberal education consists in its ability to prepare its students for a whole range of careers and occupations? By justifying the liberal arts in practical terms, we have changed the liberal arts into their opposite, into a type of training useful for the real, productive education that comes later.

These arguments for the "usefulness" of the liberal arts are omnipresent in higher education. It is the straw that contemporary liberal education grasps at because it not only has lost much of the ability to defend the liberal arts on their own terms but because it feels compelled, in the modern world, to say that these arts are, despite their nature and pedigree, truly "productive" after all. We live in America where, as we noted, we all work, and where the useful is esteemed above the academic. If we were educating a leisured class, if we were educating plantation owners and nobility or lords and landed gentry, we could rest content with notions of learning for its own sake. But this is America, and we no longer know how to make the argument and make it convincingly.

Defenders of the liberal arts are forced to make arguments for the usefulness and productivity of the liberal arts because, in America, no other argument will do. Material prosperity, technological progress, medical advances, scientific discovery, and personal comfort have been some of the goals and achievements of this nation. But progress in the material realm is not the business of the liberal arts and was never meant to be. Progress and production is the business of America, which explains the tenuous nature of liberal education in America and why education in the useful and productive arts is so clearly prized. What a society favors, it will reward. While we might fondly remember our old high school English teacher or the professor who opened our eyes to the amazing things that happened in history, rewards and praise go more readily to those who invent, build, cure, or who make employment possible for many. It is no wonder that the vocational arts rather than the liberal arts have such wide and deep appeal.

So the arts that most benefit society are not, it would seem, the liberal arts, but the useful arts: doing, producing, inventing, growing, and selling. To study a trade, say electronics repair, or a profession, say dentistry, is to nurture a vocation and to gain the wherewithal to do a job. Conversely, to study philosophy or ancient Greek is "liberal." But, to be blunt, why should the country care that Suzy or Joe are studying Greek? The well-trained electrician is a real benefit to hundreds of families, while the well-trained classicist may well be merely a curiosity. Even the fine arts, which give adornment to the world and enjoyment to its people, have an easier case to make than the liberal arts. So far, in any contest among the useful, the fine, and the liberal arts, it looks like the liberal arts are coming in third.

So, unless the liberal arts can show why and how they truly are of real value—not "use," but *value*—to society as well as to the individual, most American students will rightly look upon them as more or less a waste of time.

At this juncture I know there are some who are tempted to say,

> Screw society. The important thing about the liberal arts is that it empowers ME. It *frees me* from common opinion, it liberates me from the ignorance of ordinary men, it opens up a whole world of critical thinking *for me*. A liberal education is an aristocratic, *private* education par excellence: It teaches me, as Socrates showed, to scoff at superstition and put aside mere opinion, to disdain appearances and zero in on the essence of things, to be a thinker liberated from society's orthodoxies.

How many educators believe that—that the real value of the liberal arts is that it teaches us how to be little Socrateses, questioners of all things, smashers of all idols, cynics-for-rent both on college campuses and at large?

The attempt to make the liberal arts the acid that corrodes the ordinary and liberates young minds from the traditional or religious, or from the beliefs of their parents or society, is a pinched and truncated view of the liberal arts. It is hardly the traditional view of our studies, that have far more to do with wonder and gaining insight into the most important human issues, than it has to do with being critical or unorthodox. And it is essentially the reason why liberal education—especially the humanities part of liberal education—is often held in such contempt by so many ordinary citizens. A haughty sociologist or literary theorist is not better, either as a man or a citizen, than those who study medicine or engineering or farming or nursing . . . and everybody knows it except the haughty liberal artist. Nor was this view of the liberal arts even close to how the Founders viewed their liberal education. If such an education was not productive of good character or useful to their country and their fellow citizens, it had, to them, little use and scant value at all.

To defend the liberal arts *in America* we cannot recreate a quasi-aristocratic defense of it, saying that it is of private value, "useless" in any ordinary sense of the word, empowering me and me alone. Nor will it do to say that we few, we happy few, study the liberating arts while the many are either forced or fit to study the servile arts, learning how to make a living while doing the bidding of others. Haughtiness and arrogance ill befit a course of study that today needs all the friends it can find.

Oddly, the liberal arts have potential allies everywhere, if only we knew how to approach them. Yes, I know, one can make more money majoring in business than in literature. But few of us would give into the idea that we humans are so tyrannized over by economics that we give other goods no thought. How false is that, especially, when it comes to young minds, young adults of college age.

The simple truth is that there are things in compendium of the liberal arts that most students would like to know, even if their teachers have not been able to show them the connections very well. Our students may, along with Sam Cooke, not know much about their science book or the French they took, but they almost always would like to know more about love and friendship, betrayal and obligation; they do want to know something about who they are and how they fit into their societies. Once, there was hope that the humanities might help them see these objects more clearly, but now it's harder. "I didn't know you could learn about love from Shakespeare," I once heard a young woman say, "For that I thought you had to go to the movies."

Americans have lost sight of the true excellence of the liberal arts. Having decided that the liberal arts, especially the humanities, should no longer answer these longings but now have more critical and interpretive issues to address—academic issues, graduate school type issues, ideological issues, group-esteem and group identification issues—colleges have abandoned the liberal arts at their best and substituted their own narrow social or academic concerns. This failure to help students come to understand the possibilities latent in the deepest questions they want to ask is part of the sadness of higher education today, the contemporary betrayal of our students by the intellectual class.

Finally, consider the Founders' connection to the liberal arts. While one might have thought that America's Founders, an eminently practical bunch, would have been squarely on the side of practicality and practical education, this is not exactly the case. As noted previously, the writings of the Founders are littered with references to ancient Rome and Athens, or to Demosthenes and Cicero or Plutarch and Aristotle, or to the political histories of places as far-flung as Persia and Poland or San Marino and Sparta or Carthage and Thebes. These were living examples that informed their understanding not only of historical truths or political forms but also of human types and human psychology. Solon, Blackstone, Priestly, Locke, Hume . . . even such now obscure items as the Phocians, the Amphictyonic League, and the Aulic Council of the Holy Roman Empire were there for instruction and example.

The Federalist Papers are no different. Under the name of Publius (whom they read about in Plutarch) are references to everything from Alexander the Great, Aratus, and the nine archons of Athens to the Union of Utrecht, Xerxes, and Zaleucus, founder of the Locrians. (Bear in mind that these essays were first published in the newspapers. Try doing that these days.)

Remarkably, the Founders put their learning to practical *use*. For it seems that the Founders had no time for the view that liberal learning was somehow just "for its own sake" and not for application or "use." The liberal arts existed to give shape and clarity to strong minds, to give us *insights* into the most important things in the world, and to show us how to use this arsenal of stupendous knowledge to do the most important thing—not to spend our leisure in the quiet enjoyment of private wisdom but to lead a whole nation. In this regard consider Hamilton's comment in the very first *Federalist*:

> It has been frequently remarked that it seems to have been reserved to the people of this country, by their conduct and example, to decide the important question, whether societies of men are really capable or not of establishing good government from reflection and choice, or whether they are forever destined to depend for their political constitutions on accident and force.[8]

"Reflection and choice" rather than "accident and force." We would not be a nation shaped by outside conquest or fated by its past. We would reflect on what was best and then make our choice accordingly. But what is the promise of the liberal arts other than the ability to reflect and, then, to choose? What more than to survey the history of human lives and makings, to read moral and political philosophy, to read the book of human nature and see the workings of virtue and vice, ambition and altruism, wisdom and foolishness? What were they debating in Philadelphia other than the pitfalls and promise of democracy versus monarchy versus aristocratic forms? Or the degree to which human nature could be relied on or not? Or the historic examples of confederacies that succeeded and those that failed? Or the right relation of liberty and power? What were they doing in Philadelphia other than thinking through our future with the sharpest tools they had—their readings and their books? It is the liberal arts that help free us, both individually and together, from the tyranny of accident and force, and give us the ability to make more rational and, yes, more practical choices.

It was not practicality *per se* that the Founders were arguing over in 1787. It was History, Philosophy, Politics, Law, Psychology, and the Classics. And it was not a nation resting on blood or ancestry, history or traditions, which they raised up. Rather, it was a country that took seriously the examples and arguments given to it in its books, upon which we then thought, argued, and chose. The liberal arts had a far greater function than personal edification or private delight. They had, indeed, the greatest of public uses. To see the practical powers of the liberal arts, we need only to look at their ability to inform statesmen, who, upon that basis, could and did raise up a wholly new nation.

If this is true, let me be so bold as to say that America's founding in "reflection and choice" makes the United States the world's first, and perhaps the world's only, Liberal Arts Nation.

The theme of this essay has been to show that there was in this country, once, a species of what we call the liberal arts that was vital and vibrant, productive not only of smart people with penetrating thoughts but those who were productive of actual and widespread good. If, because of our ingrained prejudice, we still resist saying the liberal arts are "of use" let's at least say they can be of value—of, indeed, inestimable value.

Nevertheless, not everything that passes today for the liberal arts looks like the liberal arts of the Founding or even the liberal arts of fifty years ago. Let us not be deceived by names. To be clear, this chapter is *not* a defense of the liberal arts, especially of the humanities, as practiced in the vast majority of today's universities and colleges.

Those are the obvious conclusions of this chapter. Here are a few less obvious conclusions:

First, while most of the greatest statesmen of the Founding generation were highly liberally educated, the obvious exception was George Washington. But if Washington could be the indispensible leader of America while lacking what we generally think of as a liberal education, we in the academy at least have to rethink the possibilities of professional and vocational education to make generous, intelligent, and prudent gentlemen and statesmen. Indeed, we in the academy have to do all we can to praise the honest good that such an education brings to the vast majority of students today, and do all we can to improve it. Did Jefferson ever argue that his technical, agricultural, and mechanical learning were of lesser consequence than his liberal education, or that those studies did little to give shape and valued content to his mind? I think not.

Second, those who do not know how to contribute to the improvement of vocational or professional education should at least have the decency to get out of the way.

Third, if Madison is a model of a liberally educated statesman, consider the character of his education and how it might relate to what is termed the liberal arts today. Would he have been more liberally educated if he went to Princeton today, sampled its general education requirements, then "majored" in political science and "minored" in . . . well, what? What was the character of liberal education back then that enabled it to produce insightful statesmen versus the current products of our variety of liberal education. Literary critics? "Humanists"? Dilettantes? Professors?

Fourth, consider the notion that the liberal arts and liberal arts education are not the same thing. For example, in considering the comparison of Lincoln with Everett, might not the lesson be that there is nothing much wrong with the real liberal arts and everything wrong with how we teach them? The liberal arts did not make Edward Everett irrelevant, though perhaps his education did. And education did not make Lincoln the statesman he surely was, though the insights garnered from the study of the liberal arts surely did.

Fifth, the Founders' and Lincoln's liberal arts do not have to be *forced* to be civic or pushed to teach patriotism. Real issues examined through the lens of the greatest accumulated wisdom, real concerns parsed by great minds, real history taught and absorbed, real science strengthening the powers of mind and insight, real literature strengthening the imagination . . . all these together helping to shape the minds of our fellow citizens to make reasonable choices and pick thoughtful and broadly educated leaders—that is civic virtue aplenty. I am experienced enough to know that to teach our students the insights of the Founding is enough to make them respect this nation and be devoted to it. Compared to that, patriotism without knowledge is merely a false love, and it will crumple at the first attack.

NOTES

1. U.S. Constitution (1787), art. 1, sec. 8, clause 8, wherein Congress is empowered "To promote the Progress of Science and useful Arts, by securing for limited Times to Authors and Inventors the exclusive Right to their respective Writings and Discoveries."

2. See Eugene F. Miller, "On the American Founders' Defense of Liberal Education in a Republic," *The Review of Politics* 46, no. 1 (January 1984): 78–79. See also Frederick

Rudolph, ed., *Essays on Education in the Early Republic* (Cambridge, MA: Harvard University Press, 1965).

3. Quoted in Viola A. Conklin, *American Political History to the Death of Lincoln* (New York: Henry Holt, 1901), 10.

4. Alexis de Tocqueville, *Democracy in America*, 2 vols. (1835; New York: Vintage Classics, 1990), 2:37, 39, 42, 45, 48.

5. On Lincoln's reading, see Robert Bray, "What Abraham Lincoln Read—An Evaluative and Annotated List," *Journal of the Abraham Lincoln Association* 28 (Summer 2007): 28–81; Robert Bray, *Reading with Lincoln* (Carbondale: Southern Illinois University Press, 2010).

6. Consider Lincoln's own description of his education: "It was a wild region, with many bears and other wild animals still in the woods. There I grew up. There were some schools, so called; but no qualification was ever required of a teacher, beyond '*readin, writin*, and *cipherin*,' to the Rule of Three. If a straggler supposed to understand latin happened to sojourn in the neighborhood, he was looked upon as a wizzard. There was absolutely nothing to excite ambition for education. Of course when I came of age I did not know much. Still somehow, I could read, write, and cipher to the Rule of Three; but that was all. I have not been to school since. The little advance I now have upon this store of education, I have picked up from time to time under the pressure of necessity." See Lincoln to Jesse W. Fell, December 20, 1859, in Roy P. Basler et al., eds., *The Collected Works of Abraham Lincoln*, 9 vols. (New Brunswick, NJ: Rutgers University Press, 1953–1955), 3:511.

7. For more on the speeches at Gettysburg, see Garry Wills, *Lincoln at Gettysburg: The Words that Remade America* (New York: Simon & Schuster, 1992).

8. Alexander Hamilton, *Federalist* No. 1.

Afterword

The Impoverishment of American Culture

Dana Gioia

At heart I am still a working-class kid—half Italian, half Mexican—from Los Angeles, or more precisely from Hawthorne, a city most often remembered as the setting of Quentin Tarantino's *Pulp Fiction* and *Jackie Brown*—two films that capture the ineffable charm of my hometown. I am the first person in my family ever to attend college, and I owe my education to my father, who sacrificed nearly everything to give his four children the best education possible. My dad had a fairly hard life. He never spoke English until he went to school. He barely survived a plane crash in World War II. He worked hard, but never had much success, except with his family. When I was about 12 years old, my dad told me that he hoped I would go to Stanford University, a place I had never heard of. For him, Stanford represented every success he had missed yet wanted for his children. He would be proud of me today.

On the other hand, my mother could be a challenge. For example, when she learned that I had been nominated to be chairman of the National Endowment for the Arts, she phoned and said, "Don't think I'm impressed."

There was a bit of controversy when my name was announced as Stanford's graduation speaker in 2007. A few students were especially concerned that I lacked celebrity status. It seemed I was not famous enough. I could not agree more. As I have often told my wife and children, "I'm simply not famous enough." And that—in a more general and less personal sense—is the subject I want to address, the fact that we live in a culture that barely acknowledges and rarely celebrates the arts or artists.

There is an experiment I would love to conduct. I would like to survey a cross-section of Americans and ask them how many active NBA players, Major League Baseball players, and *American Idol* finalists they can name. Then I would ask them how many living American poets, playwrights, painters, sculptors, architects, classical musicians, conductors, and composers they can name. I would even like to ask how many living American scientists or social thinkers they can name.

Fifty years ago, I suspect that along with Mickey Mantle, Willie Mays, and Sandy Koufax, most Americans could have named, at the very least, Robert Frost, Carl Sandburg, Arthur Miller, Thornton Wilder, Georgia O'Keeffe, Leonard Bernstein, Leontyne Price, and Frank Lloyd Wright. Not to mention scientists and thinkers like Linus Pauling, Jonas Salk, Rachel Carson, Margaret Mead, and especially Dr. Alfred Kinsey.

I do not think that Americans were smarter then, but American culture was. Even the mass media placed a greater emphasis on presenting a broad range of human achievement.

I grew up mostly among immigrants, many of whom never learned to speak English. But at night watching TV variety programs like the *Ed Sullivan Show* or the *Perry Como Music Hall*, I saw—along with comedians, popular singers, and movie stars—classical musicians like Jascha Heifetz and Arthur Rubinstein, opera singers like Robert Merrill and Anna Moffo, and jazz greats like Duke Ellington and Louis Armstrong captivate an audience of millions with their art.

The same was even true of literature. I first encountered Robert Frost, John Steinbeck, Lillian Hellman, and James Baldwin on general interest television shows. All of these people were famous to the average American—because the culture considered them important.

Today no working-class or immigrant kid would encounter that range of arts and ideas in the popular culture. Almost everything in our national culture—even the news—has been reduced to entertainment, or altogether eliminated.

The loss of recognition for artists, thinkers, and scientists has impoverished our culture in innumerable ways, but let me mention one. When virtually all of a culture's celebrated figures are in sports or entertainment, how few possible role models we offer the young.

There are so many other ways to lead a successful and meaningful life that are not denominated by money or fame. Adult life begins in a child's imagination, and we have relinquished that imagination to the marketplace.

Of course, I'm not forgetting that politicians can also be famous, but it is interesting how our political process grows more like the entertainment industry each year. When a successful guest appearance on the *Colbert Report* becomes more important than passing legislation, democracy gets scary. No wonder Hollywood considers politics "show business for ugly people."

Everything now is entertainment. And the purpose of this omnipresent commercial entertainment is to sell us something. American culture has mostly become one vast infomercial.

I have a recurring nightmare. I am in Rome visiting the Sistine Chapel. I look up at Michelangelo's incomparable fresco of the "Creation of Man." I see God stretching out his arm to touch the reclining Adam's finger. And then I notice in the other hand Adam is holding a Diet Pepsi.

When was the last time you have seen a featured guest on *David Letterman* or *Jay Leno* who isn't trying to sell you something? A new movie, a new TV show, a new book, or a new vote?

Don't get me wrong. I love entertainment, and I love the free market. I have a Stanford MBA and spent fifteen years in the food industry. I adore my big-screen TV. The productivity and efficiency of the free market is beyond dispute. It has created a society of unprecedented prosperity.

But we must remember that the marketplace does only one thing—it puts a price on everything. The role of culture, however, must go beyond economics. It is not focused on the price of things, but on their value. And, above all, culture should tell us what is beyond price, including what does not belong in the marketplace. A culture should also provide some cogent view of the good life beyond mass accumulation. In this respect, our culture is failing us.

There is only one social force in America potentially large and strong enough to counterbalance this profit-driven commercialization of cultural values, our educational system, especially public education. Traditionally, education has been one thing that our nation has agreed cannot be left entirely to the marketplace—but made mandatory and freely available to everyone.

At 56, I am just old enough to remember a time when every public high school in this country had a music program with choir and band, usually a jazz band, too, sometimes even orchestra. And every high school offered a drama program, sometimes with dance instruction. And there were writing opportunities in the school paper and literary magazine, as well as studio art training. I'm sorry to say that these programs are no longer widely available to the new generation of Americans. This once visionary and democratic system has been almost entirely dismantled by well-meaning but myopic school boards, county commissioners, and state officials, with the federal government largely indifferent to the issue. Art became an expendable luxury, and 50 million students have paid the price. Today a child's access to arts education is largely a function of his or her parents' income.

In a time of social progress and economic prosperity, why have we experienced this colossal cultural and political decline? There are several reasons, but I must risk offending many friends and colleagues by saying that surely artists and intellectuals are partly to blame. Most American artists, intellectuals, and academics have lost their ability to converse with the rest of society. We have become wonderfully expert in talking to one another, but we have become almost invisible and inaudible in the general culture.

This mutual estrangement has had enormous cultural, social, and political consequences. America needs its artists and intellectuals, and they need to reestablish their rightful place in the general culture. If we could reopen the conversation between our best minds and the broader public, the results would not only transform society but also artistic and intellectual life.

There is no better place to start this rapprochement than in arts education. How do we explain to the larger society the benefits of this civic investment when the public has become convinced that the purpose of arts education is mostly to produce more artists—hardly a compelling argument to either the average taxpayer or financially strapped school board?

We need to create a new national consensus. The purpose of arts education is not to produce more artists, though that is a byproduct. The real purpose of arts education is to create complete human beings capable of leading successful and productive lives in a free society.

This is not happening now in American schools. Even if we forget the larger catastrophe that only 70 percent of American kids now graduate from high school, what are we to make of a public education system whose highest goal seems to be producing minimally competent entry-level workers?

The situation is a cultural and educational disaster, but it also has huge and alarming economic consequences. If the United States is to compete effectively with the rest of the world in the new global marketplace, it is not going to succeed through cheap labor or cheap raw materials, nor even the free flow of capital or a streamlined industrial base. To compete successfully, this country needs continued creativity, ingenuity, and innovation.

It is hard to see those qualities thriving in a nation whose educational system ranks at the bottom of the developed world and has mostly eliminated the arts from the curriculum. I have seen firsthand the enormous transformative power of the arts—in the lives of individuals, in communities, and even society at large. Marcus Aurelius believed that the course of wisdom consisted of learning to trade easy pleasures for more complex and challenging ones. I worry about a culture that bit by bit trades off the challenging pleasures of art for the easy comforts of entertainment. And that is exactly what is happening—not just in the media, but in our schools and civic life.

Entertainment promises us a predictable pleasure—humor, thrills, emotional titillation, or even the odd delight of being vicariously terrified. It exploits and manipulates who we are rather than challenges us with a vision of who we might become. A child who spends a month mastering *Halo* or *NBA Live* on Xbox has not been awakened and transformed the way that child would be spending the time rehearsing a play or learning to draw.

Recent statistical studies on American civic participation confirm this point. Our country is dividing into two distinct behavioral groups. One group spends most of its free time sitting at home as passive consumers of electronic entertainment. Even family communication is breaking down as members increasingly spend their time alone, staring at their individual screens. The other group also uses and enjoys the new technology, but these individuals balance it with a broader range of activities. They go out—to exercise, play sports, volunteer and do charity work at about three times the level of the first group. By every measure they are vastly more active and socially engaged than the first group.

What is the defining difference between passive and active citizens? Curiously, it is not income, geography, or even education. It depends on whether or not they read for pleasure and participate in the arts. These cultural activities seem to awaken a heightened sense of individual awareness and social responsibility.

Why do these issues matter? Because this is the culture that American college students enter upon graduation. For four years, while attending college, they not only study, but are also part of a community that takes arts and ideas seriously. Even if they spent most of their free time watching *Grey's Anatomy*, playing *Guitar Hero*, or Facebooking their friends, those important endeavors are balanced by courses and conversations about literature, politics, technology, and ideas. But when they graduate this support system ends and they now face the choice of whether they want to be passive consumers or active citizens. They must decide whether they will watch the world on a screen or live in it so meaningfully that they change it.

That is no easy task, so we must not forget what the arts provide.

Art is an irreplaceable way of understanding and expressing the world—equal to but distinct from scientific and conceptual methods. Art addresses us in the fullness of our being—simultaneously speaking to our intellect, emotions, intuition, imagination, memory, and physical senses. There are some truths about life that can only be expressed as a story, or a song, or an image.

Art delights, instructs, consoles. It educates our emotions. And it remembers. As Robert Frost once said about poetry, "It is a way of remembering that which it would impoverish us to forget." Art awakens, enlarges, refines, and restores our humanity. You don't outgrow art. The same work can mean something different at each stage of your life. A good book changes as you change.

Adapted from Dana Gioia's address delivered at Stanford University's 116th Commencement on June 17, 2007.

Index

common good, 16, 18, 27, 50, 52–53, 54,
    112, 122
common school, 8, 15–32
Conrad, Joseph, 130
Constitution, U.S., 2, 2–3, 7, 8, 42,
    44–45, 49, 68, 69, 73, 74, 92, 93, 106,
    117, 132, 134–135, 139
Constitutional Convention, 15
Cooke, Sam, 146
Counts, George, 31, 32
A Crucible Moment, 4
culture wars, 20
curriculum, 16, 25, 27, 28, 28–29, 30, 32,
    68, 69, 72, 154; core curriculum, 17,
    25, 30, 120, 149
Curti, Merle, 8

Dawkins, Richard, 98
Declaration of Independence, 1–2, 3,
    16, 44, 68, 69, 74, 135
Delattre, Edwin J. (president, St. John's
    College), 125
democracy, 4, 8, 18, 19, 23, 27, 38, 49,
    56, 132, 141, 147, 152. *See also*
    republic/republicanism; voting
Democracy in America, 18. *See also*
    Tocqueville, Alexis de
Department of Education, 69, 70, 165
Dewey, John, 127
Digital Age, 85, 88, 104, 135
Dos Passos, John, 37
Douglass, Frederick, 2
Dunn, Anita, 99

education: child-centered, 8, 27, 28–29,
    29, 30, 31, 32; civic, 4, 5, 8, 10, 49, 51,
    52, 60, 61, 91, 132; elementary,
    16–17, 18, 70; liberal, 8, 117, 128, 129,
    134, 139, 140, 142, 144, 145, 148, 149;
    moral, 53; progressive, 31–32;
    public, 3, 8–9, 24, 70, 127, 152, 154;
    secondary, 83, 127, 133, 135, 136;
    undergraduate, 4, 5, 6, 20, 38, 39, 44,
    68, 70, 71, 73, 82, 87, 111, 112, 114,
    115, 116, 117, 118, 118–119, 120, 126,
    127, 128, 131, 133, 134, 136, 139, 140,
    143, 144, 145, 146, 148, 151
Eisenhower, Dwight D., 96
Ellington, Duke, 152

Eliot, George, 130
Emerson, Ralph Waldo, 39
Enlightenment, 3, 7, 19, 49, 51, 134
equality, 16–17, 20, 21, 26, 27, 54, 56,
    117
Erasmus, 126
ESPN Magazine, 81
Euclid, 141
Euripides, 141
Everett, Edward, 141, 149

Facebook, 79, 81, 86, 88, 100, 155
faction, 16, 92
Faulkner, William, 67
Federal Election Commission (FEC),
    102, 102–103
The Federalist Papers, 69, 70, 139, 147
Federalists, 50
First Amendment, 19, 86–87, 106, 112
Ford, Henry, 40
Founding generation, 3, 73, 139, 140,
    148. *See also* American Founding
Foxworthy, Jeff, 7
Franklin, Benjamin, 3, 4, 15–16, 17, 74,
    83, 140
free press. *See* First Amendment
free speech. *See* First Amendment
freedom of association. *See* First
    Amendment
French and Indian War, 69, 70
Froebel, Friedrich, 31
Frost, Robert, 152, 155

Gandhi, Mahatma, 130
Garland, Rebecca, 67
Gettysburg, 45, 141
Gioia, Dana, 6, 10
Glorious Revolution, 57
Goheen, Robert (president, Princeton
    University), 136
Google, 88, 118
grade inflation, 111
Grigsby, Mary, 5

Hamilton, Alexander, 50, 147
Harry Potter, 81, 83
Harvard University, 22, 29, 38, 120, 141
Heclo, Hugh, 92, 95
Heifetz, Jascha, 152

About the Editors and Contributors

EDITORS

Elizabeth Kaufer Busch is associate professor of American studies at Christopher Newport University and founder and co-director of the Center for American Studies (CAS), an independent center formed to respond to the growing lack of civic literacy among college students and citizens. Busch earned her Ph.D. in political science from Michigan State University with specializations in modern and American political thought. In 2007, Busch co-authored and was awarded a "We The People" Challenge Grant from the National Endowment for the Humanities to support CAS. Her research focuses on American political thought, the U.S. governmental system, and the evolution of women's movements in America. She has published articles, book chapters, and scholarly studies on these subjects and is co-editor of *Democracy Revisited: Essays on the American Regime* (Lexington Books, 2009).

Jonathan W. White is assistant professor of American studies at Christopher Newport University. He earned his Ph.D. in U.S. history from the University of Maryland at College Park and has published numerous articles about Abraham Lincoln and the Civil War in scholarly journals and popular history magazines. He is the recipient of the 2010 Hay-Nicolay Dissertation Prize, which is awarded jointly by the Abraham Lincoln Institute and the Abraham Lincoln Association, and he is the author of *Abraham Lincoln and Treason in the Civil War: The Trials of John Merryman* (2011).

CONTRIBUTORS

John Agresto has held numerous prestigious academic posts both in America and around the world, including provost and academic dean at the American University of Iraq in Sulaimani, visiting fellow at the Madison Program in American Ideals and Institutions at Princeton University, senior advisor for Higher Education and Scientific Research for the Coalition Provisional Authority in Iraq, president of St. John's College in Santa Fe, Lily Senior Research Fellow at Wabash College, and acting chairman of the National Endowment for the Humanities. He has also taught at the

University of Toronto, Kenyon College, Duke University and the New School University. Agresto is the author or editor of five books, including *Mugged by Reality: The Liberation of Iraq and the Failure of Good Intentions* (2007), *The Supreme Court and Constitutional Democracy* (1984), *The Humanist as Citizen: Essays on the Uses of the Humanities* (1981), and, most recently, *Tomatoes, Basil, and Olive Oil: An Italian-American Cookbook* (2011).

Mark Bauerlein earned his doctorate in English at UCLA in 1988. He has taught at Emory University since 1989, with a two-and-a-half year break in 2003–2005 to serve as the director of the Office of Research and Analysis at the National Endowment for the Arts. Apart from his scholarly work, Bauerlein publishes in popular periodicals such as the *Wall Street Journal*, the *Weekly Standard*, the *Washington Post*, *TLS*, and the *Chronicle of Higher Education*. His latest book, *The Dumbest Generation: How the Digital Age Stupefies Young Americans and Jeopardizes Our Future; Or, Don't Trust Anyone Under 30*, was published in 2008.

Jeff Bergner received his B.A. from Carleton College and M.A. and Ph.D. degrees from Princeton University. He has taught at the University of Pennsylvania, the University of Michigan, Georgetown University, and Christopher Newport University. He served as chief of staff to a U.S. senator, staff director of the Senate Foreign Relations Committee, and as Assistant Secretary of State. He is the author or co-author of five books, including *Branding the Candidate: Marketing Strategies to Win Your Vote* (2011), an in-depth study of the 2008 presidential election campaign. He has written dozens of scholarly articles, opinion pieces, and newspaper columns, and speaks regularly on American politics and international affairs.

Peter A. Benoliel earned his B.A. in philosophy from Princeton University. After serving three years in the U.S. Navy, he joined Quaker Chemical Corporation as a chemist in 1957. In 1966, he was appointed president and CEO of the company, serving in that capacity until 1992. Benoliel has served on a number of corporate boards over the years in addition to serving as chairman of the Federal Reserve Bank of Philadelphia from 1989 to 1992. He has also been active in many cultural and philanthropic organizations, serving as chair of the United Way of Southeastern Pennsylvania, the Philadelphia Orchestra Association, and the Free Library of Philadelphia Foundation, and on the boards of the National Humanities Center, St. John's College, the Philadelphia Museum of Art, the Library Company of Philadelphia, as well as a number of music schools and organizations.

Bruce Cole is a senior fellow at the Ethics and Public Policy Center in Washington, D.C. He served as chairman of the National Endowment for

the Humanities from 2001 to 2009 and as president and CEO of the American Revolution Center from 2009 to 2012. Before heading the NEH, Cole was Distinguished Professor of Art History and professor of comparative literature at Indiana University in Bloomington. He is the author of fourteen books and numerous articles and has held fellowships and grants from, among others, the Guggenheim Foundation, the American Council of Learned Societies, the Kress Foundation, the American Philosophical Society, and the Center for Medieval and Renaissance Studies at the University of California, Los Angeles. In November 2008, President George W. Bush awarded Cole the Presidential Citizens Medal "for his work to strengthen our national memory and ensure that our country's heritage is passed on to future generations."

Dana Gioia is an internationally acclaimed and award-winning poet and is the Judge Widney Professor of Poetry and Public Culture at the University of Southern California. He received a B.A. and M.B.A. from Stanford University and an M.A. in comparative literature from Harvard University. Gioia has published four full-length collections of poetry, as well as eight chapbooks. His poetry collection, *Interrogations at Noon*, won the 2002 American Book Award. An influential critic as well, Gioia's 1991 volume *Can Poetry Matter?* is credited with helping to revive the role of poetry in American public culture. His work has appeared in many magazines including *The New Yorker, The Atlantic, The Washington Post Book World, The New York Times Book Review, Slate,* and *The Hudson Review*. As chairman of the National Endowment for the Arts (2002–2009), Gioia succeeded in garnering bipartisan support in Congress for the mission of the NEA and in strengthening the national consensus in favor of public funding for the arts, arts education, and literacy.

E. D. Hirsch, Jr., is the Linden Kent Memorial Professor of English Emeritus at the University of Virginia. He is the author of several acclaimed books on education issues including the *New York Times* bestseller *Cultural Literacy* (1991), *The Schools We Need and Why We Don't Have Them,* which was recognized by the *New York Times* as one of its "Notable Books of 1996," and *The Making of Americans: Democracy and Our Schools* (2009). Additional works by Hirsch include *The Knowledge Deficit, Books to Build On* (co-editor), *The Dictionary of Cultural Literacy,* and the best-selling Core Knowledge series which begins with *What Your Kindergartner Needs to Know* and continues through each grade, concluding with *What Your Sixth Grader Needs to Know*. Hirsch is an elected member of both the American Academy of Arts and Sciences and the International Academy of Education. He has served on the Research Advisory Board of the U.S. Department of Education and, in 1997, received the Biennial Quest Award for Outstanding Contribution to Education from the American Federation of Teachers.

Wilfred M. McClay is SunTrust Bank Chair of Excellence in Humanities and professor of history at the University of Tennessee at Chattanooga. He was appointed in 2002 to the National Council on the Humanities, the advisory board for the National Endowment for the Humanities. His book *The Masterless: Self and Society in Modern America* won the 1995 Merle Curti Award of the Organization of American Historians for the best book in American intellectual history. Among his other books are *The Student's Guide to U.S. History*, *Religion Returns to the Public Square: Faith and Policy in America*, and *Figures in the Carpet: Finding the Human Person in the American Past*. He has been the recipient of fellowships from the Woodrow Wilson International Center for Scholars, the National Endowment for the Humanities, and the National Academy of Education. McClay was educated at St. John's College (Annapolis) and the Johns Hopkins University and has taught at Tulane University, Pepperdine University, the University of Rome, Georgetown University, and the University of Dallas.

Andrea Radasanu is assistant professor of political science at Northern Illinois University specializing in early liberal thought. She has published articles and book chapters on several thinkers including Montesquieu, Burke, and Rousseau and is the editor of *The Pious Sex: Essays on Women and Religion in the History of Political Thought* (Lexington Books, 2010). She is currently completing a book manuscript on Montesquieu's international relations thought.

Lisa Spiller is professor of marketing at Christopher Newport University, where she has taught for more than twenty-five years. She has won numerous awards for her teaching and scholarship and is co-author of the widely acclaimed textbook *Contemporary Direct and Interactive Marketing*, which has been used by colleges and universities in thirty-four states and six countries. Her research has been published in many academic journals and textbooks. Most recently, she is co-author of *Branding the Candidate: Marketing Strategies to Win Your Vote* (2011).

Jonathan Yonan is dean of the Templeton Honors College at Eastern University. He earned a D.Phil. in ecclesiastical history at Oxford University, writing his dissertation on religious nonconformists and religious toleration in the eighteenth-century transatlantic world.